To our dear friends
Sheyda

I hope you ,
book and in some small
way it contributes to
a better world for
our kids.

# HOW TO SAVE
# THE WORLD
# ON $5 A DAY

xo
Fred and
Margie

2/16/13

# HOW TO SAVE THE WORLD

# ON $5 A DAY

*A PARABLE OF*

*PERSONAL PHILANTHROPY*

BY

FRED LAWRENCE FELDMAN

# CONTENTS

# INTRODUCTION

This book will help you improve your sense of wellbeing and your outlook on life through acts of charity.

If you already give to charities, I salute you for your generosity and I believe this book will show you how to leverage your altruism to tap ever-greater wellsprings of satisfaction through a process I call *Personal Philanthropy*.

If you don't currently contribute, this book will introduce you to the profound benefits to be had when you – like the characters in the parable you're about to read – become introduced to personal philanthropy as the way to master the art of giving.

In the interest of honest disclosure, let me say that I'm a creative consultant who has partnered with nonprofit organizations for over twenty years. I've helped raise millions of dollars on behalf of such charities as the Arthritis Foundation, the Alzheimer's Association, Habitat for Humanity, Volunteers of America, and many others.

I love that in some way I've helped to make the world a better place... and that every day I can feel good about myself despite all my petty failings and shortcoming, failures and frustrations, because I'm taking part in something meaningful and important. You, too, can have this sense of wellbeing – whether you have five dollars or five million dollars to contribute, or just an hour or two of your time.

Zen masters put forth that enlightenment comes through remembering what we already know. What we already *know* but may have *forgotten* about giving is that when we make a charitable donation we are simply *doing a favor.*

We certainly feel good about ourselves when we do a favor for family or friends. We should feel the same satisfaction when we give to a charitable cause.

For many of us, however, charitable giving is no longer perceived as a privilege and a pleasure but a duty that provides us with about as much satisfaction as dashing off a check to the electric company. Charitable giving has become merely another obligatory chore during our busy day – that is, if we give at all.

That's a terrible loss, because our potential to enjoy giving is what sets us apart from virtually every other species on the planet. (Yes, other creatures are driven by instinct to act in ways that resemble self-sacrifice on behalf of the herd or their young but only people can *choose* to give, and only we can *feel good* about it!)

Think back to the last time you bought a box of cookies or a chocolate bar from the kid next door who was participating in a fundraiser, or when you dropped a few coins into a trick-or-treater's UNICEF box on Halloween…

I'd wager that giving in *those* circumstances put a smile on your face and lightened your heart…

You can experience that same one-to-one immediacy and be touched and nourished on psychological and emotional levels whenever you give, even if you only write a check or make an online credit card donation. You can prosper in mind, body and spirit by perfecting the art of personal philanthropy, as you'll discover in **How to Save the World on $5 a Day.**

"Everyone thinks of changing the world, but no one thinks of changing himself."

—Tolstoy

"Unless someone like you cares a whole awful lot, nothing is going to get better. It's not."

—Dr. Seuss

# 1. RECIPE FOR A BETTER REALITY

In a city built upon a river, in a shabby neighborhood, it was 8 AM on a weekday morning at the youth center. A wind-driven, slanting, late spring rain rattled the window as Annette sat in her cubbyhole of an office. She was dreading the expected arrival of the construction guys, who were going to check out the center's salvageable copper and fixtures in preparation for the building's imminent demolition.

Annette shifted in her folding chair behind her battered gray metal desk. For the gizzilionth time, she let play in her head the dismal loop of her telephone conversation with the pro bono attorney, late last evening.

*"Sure, we can put up legal roadblocks to slow Bender Realty Trust down,"* the attorney told her. *"But it's just a matter of time before the wrecking ball. Bender has a lot of juice in this city..."*

*"I grew up in this neighborhood,"* Annette said. *"My roots are here, like the children of the families I serve."*

*"You've got a gang problem there, too, I understand."*

*"Yes, but thanks to this center we're making progress..."* Annette paused. *"So what you're telling me is the battle to save the youth center is over, and I've lost?"* She desperately hoped the attorney would contradict her.

*"How old are you, young lady?"*

*"Twenty-seven, why?"*

*"My law degree is older than you,"* the attorney sighed. *"I've been doing this work a long, long time, and I have to tell you, the only time I've seen David beat Goliath is in the Bible."*

On the wall of her little office, as if in commiseration of the emotional turmoil Annette was experiencing, the Kit-Kat clock ceaselessly rolled its eyes above the yellowed, dingy and ancient computer.

*Well, as long as this old place is standing, there's still hope,* Annette reminded herself. *So anything I can do to delay the end – even if the end may be inevitable – is worth doing.*

Bender's men would be here soon to survey what they could profitably rip out of the building. If she could somehow delay them, that would be time won for the youth center's survival. Even winning one more day was worth the effort because it would give her that much more time to think of an idea to once and for all save this old place infused with her heart and soul…

Annette's mother was fond of saying that there were two ways to a man's heart…

That gave Annette an idea. But it would take a few bucks to buy the ingredients to implement it. Problem was, she was flat broke.

There was always *nonno's* lucky five dollar bill, Annette thought.

*"Keep it with you always, it was good luck for your nonno during the war,"* *Nonna* Rita had proclaimed, giving the five dollar bill to Annette before she'd passed away.

That had been almost ten years ago, and Annette had kept the five dollar bill, faded and worn to the softness of flannel, gingerly folded and protected in an old pill vial. It was tucked deep in the corner of her shoulder bag.

Annette went into the kitchen, with its second hand fridge and electric range, worn red linoleum counters and pitted soapstone sink. She opened the cupboards layered thickly with mint green paint. On the shelves were a box of spaghetti, two large cans of crushed tomatoes, olive oil, salt and pepper, and plastic jars of oregano, basil, and pepper flakes. With what she might be able to buy at the bodega around the corner with her five dollars, it just could be enough…

Annette could hear the rain pelting the center's corrugated metal roof. She grabbed her yellow hooded rain slicker from the hook behind the office door and her battered and bent black umbrella.

Outside it was pouring, but it was a sultry rain, more summer-like than spring. Annette in her pink tee shirt, khaki shorts and flip-flops felt sweaty beneath the rubber rain slicker. She hurried along the cracked sidewalk with her shoulders hunched and her umbrella angled against the drenching wind. Beside her, the street's rain-slicked asphalt glistened, reflecting the ruby brake lights of the crawling traffic.

The bodega was just around the corner. As Annette made the turn she collided with a tall man in a threadbare tan trench coat striding along the middle of the sidewalk.

He was hatless, and she had but a moment to take in his long blond hair plastered to his skull by the rain, and his blue eyes, bright with *what?* – Passion? Fury? Pain? –

Then he brusquely shouldered past her without so much as an 'excuse me,' all the while muttering to himself.

*Weirdo,* Annette shrugged, closing and shaking her umbrella before stepping into the bodega Josefina ran with her husband, Miguel.

Inside, the worn, wide-board floors and wooden shelves glowed richly beneath the milk-glass light fixtures. Along the back of the store was a meat case behind which Miguel sliced cold cuts and parceled out chicken, beef, lamb and pork wrapped in crisp white paper.

In the front, by the cash register, Josefina held sway.

Despite the humidity, Josefina was bundled up in an old blue cardigan. She was in her seventies, Annette surmised. She had salt and pepper hair pulled back into a tight bun, turquoise glasses with rhinestones in the corners and a gold incisor that glinted as she welcomed Annette with a smile.

"Good morning, Annette," Josefina said warmly. "You'll see Estela this afternoon after school."

Estela, who was sixteen, was Miguel and Josefina's granddaughter. She hung out at the youth center when she wasn't working at the bodega.

Annette took a basket from the stack by the door and parsimoniously shopped, gathering an onion, a head of garlic, carrots, celery, and a pound of hamburger from Miguel behind his glass meat case. She set her would-be purchases on the counter and held her breath as Josefina totaled them up on the old black and gold cash register.

"$8.25, please," Josefina said.

Annette rummaged through her purse until her fingers touched the amber pill vial. She carefully extracted her wadded up lucky five dollar bill and spread it out on the worn wooden counter.

"Josefina, this is all I have. Do you think I can owe the rest?"

Josefina peered over the tops of her rhinestone spectacles. "Is that even real?" she fingered the bill.

Annette sighed as she realized that the bill, so worn and faded to a ghostly gray, was barely decipherable.

"My grandfather got it while he was serving in World War Two," Annette explained. "He said it brought him great good fortune."

"Like a lucky charm?" Josefina asked.

"Yes," Annette said hopefully. "I'm hoping it will bring *me* some desperately needed luck…"

She rapidly explained that the youth center was slated to be leveled, and how she hoped to delay the process as much as possible, by even one day if that's all she could manage, in the hopes of a miracle…

"That place means the world to me," Annette finished.

"I didn't know the youth center was in trouble," Josefina sighed, shaking her head. "Take that back," she gestured at the bill on the counter. "Your money's no good."

"Oh, Josefina," Annette pleaded. "It's real money, even if the bill is worn out. You don't *understand*—"

"No, child," Josefina cut her off, smiling. "It is *you* who don't understand. What I am saying is that your money's no good *here* because you can have what you want at no charge. You do so much for the neighborhood, giving Estela and her friends a place to be out of trouble after school. All of us in the community owe you a great debt."

Annette felt close to tears. "I promise I'll pay you back, Josefina," was all she could manage to say.

"Child, you already have paid us back for any kindness we may be lucky enough to be able to show you." Josefina paused. "Do you know what a *Mutualista* is?"

"No."

"We have in our culture a history of forming groups to provide support for those in our community in times of need," Josefina explained. "This group, we call it a *Mutualista*. The padre from his pulpit, he says to us the pillars of the *Mutualista* must be family, church and community. When someone you know needs help, you should whole-heartedly *give* help. *What* you can give doesn't matter nearly as much as your *intent*. It is the intent that changes things for the better."

"I'm confused about what you mean when you say that our *intent* when we give changes things for the better," Annette said.

"There is a story that is told back in Mexico by the village elders," Josefina said. "Maybe it will help you understand…

"Once there was a little peasant girl who had no money to buy a gift for the Christ Child on Christmas Eve. One by one, she watched all the wealthier children present their gifts in the village church, but she had nothing to give. Finally she gathered up a bouquet of weeds. As she lovingly selected each stem and stalk, she meditated on her love for Christ. In the Church, those who had more wealth clucked like scolding hens in the barnyard as they watched the girl place her humble offering at the foot of the Nativity scene, but all were amazed to see it transformed to the beautiful red and green of a *Flor de la Nochebuena*. This means 'Flower of the Good Night,' but here it is called a poinsettia. To this day the poinsettia is the Christmas flower, and it tells us that God looks beyond what we have to give, and measures our goodness by the amount of sharing spirit in our hearts."

"So it was God who transformed the weeds into a poinsettia?" Annette asked.

"It is one understanding of the story," Josefina agreed. "However a deeper interpretation is that it was the *little girl* who brought about the transformation of ordinary weeds into a poinsettia of great beauty. She brought about this transformation through her fierce desire to give. Her attention upon her devotion was impeccable, and so it altered her..." Josefina trailed off, looking perplexed. "Annette, what is the word in English for how we see the world?"

"Reality?" Annette offered. "You're saying the little girl changed reality through her charity?"

"I'm saying it changed *her* reality," Josefina amended. "For truly, one's own reality is all there is... The story tells us that we can transform our view of ourselves and the world – transform our 'reality' – by deeply investing ourselves in every detail of our act of charity and the feelings we experience through our giving."

Annette pondered what Josefina was saying. "My grandfather was fond of a particular biblical quote, *'Be not conformed to this world, but be transformed by the renewing of your mind, that you may prove what is the good and acceptable and perfect will of God.'*"

"Your grandfather sounds like a wise man," Josefina said. "He knew that merely going through the motions when you are giving isn't enough to bring about the transformation of reality we are speaking about. Being *mindful* and *present* during our acts of giving is what allows us to see the world with new eyes... to see our way clearly to walk with God."

"'With giving, it's the *thought* that counts,'" Annette said. "I'd always dismissed the saying as merely an old cliché, but now it seems incredibly profound..."

"It is truly a wise and deep saying," Josefina agreed. "*If* you understand the underlying meaning. Now take the food, please... And anything else you might need."

"Thank you, Josefina." Annette said, and added shyly, "Please could I also have a couple of cheese and garlic sausages, and a small bottle of your cheapest red wine?"

The storekeeper nodded. "*Anything* you need."

*I guess Nonno's lucky five dollar bill has come through once again,* Annette thought.

"Your kindness truly means the world to me," Annette said.

Josefina's gold tooth glinted as she smiled. "So, a few dollars worth of groceries is indeed small price to pay to save the world."

# #

A couple of hours later, Annette was in the youth center's kitchen, stirring the pot simmering on the stove, when the two salvage guys from Bender Realty Trust came knocking. They carried flashlights and clipboards, and wore faded jeans, scuffed tan work boots, and blue polo shirts. Their baseball caps were embroidered in yellow with the BRT logo.

"What are you cooking?" One of the men asked as soon as they were inside the door. He was a curly-haired, broad shouldered guy with a big potbelly. "It smells terrific."

"It's just *Nonna* Rita's Sunday gravy," Annette replied.

"Do I smell sausages?" The other guy asked. He was a lot smaller than his buddy, and bald, with thick glasses

"And onions, carrots, garlic, and beef," Annette agreed. "All simmered with tomatoes and red wine. I'd love to serve you guys some but it needs to cook for at least six hours…"

With her trap baited, Annette waited.

"Too bad," Curly frowned. "We'll be long gone by then."

"Hey, I have an idea," she said, striving for nonchalance. "Why don't you just come back tonight to do your survey and you can have a spaghetti dinner?"

The two workmen looked at each other. "I suppose a day one way or the other won't make much difference to Old Man Bender…," Baldy mused.

Curly nodded forcefully. "We'll see you tonight."

*Nonno's five bucks worth of luck still rules,* Annette thought triumphantly.

"You seem like a nice girl," Curly said as they were leaving. "You do realize this place is going be torn down, sooner or later, right?

"I'd rather *later*," Annette murmured.

"Pardon?" Baldy asked.

"I said, See you two *later*," she remarked sweetly. "Don't forget to bring your appetites," she added, shooing them out.

"Lady, I can see you care about this building…"

"I do."

"You realize all you're buying for yourself is a day…" Baldy began, as Annette, with a wide smile pasted on her face, shut the door.

*Another day to save her world…*

She fervently hoped that like the little Mexican girl in Josefina's story, the love in her heart and her mindfulness would be enough to change *this* reality for the better.

# 2. JOHN'S LAST DAY

At 8:02 AM that same morning, in a cramped attic apartment just three blocks from the youth center where Annette was brooding and scheming, John sat holding his head in his hands.

He'd just awoken from a vivid and frightening dream in which he'd stepped into the street, square into the path of a speeding taxi –

*Everything next happened in a rush of sound and fury. He heard the cab's horn blaring mournfully, replaced in pitch by the frantic squeal of tires. There was a flash of yellow as the cab knifed toward him, and the driver's horrified face through the windshield. The impact sent him flying through the air to land hard on the asphalt, rolling over and over to end up spread-eagled, the sky spinning crazily above.*

*There was no pain. Shouldn't there be pain? John thought in his dream. Was the lack a good thing or bad?*

*He heard the low rumble of the idling cab, and then tires again squealing as the driver peeled out.*

*Smart move, John thought. No witnesses, so why stick around?*

*He wondered if the cabbie would at least call 911 on his behalf.*

*Probably not. They could trace those calls...*

*Above him, the sky seemed to be rapidly darkening, the vivid azure deepening to purple as that Cat Stevens refrain began hauntingly...*

*"...And if my colors all run dry..."*

*There was still no pain. Just a gradual and building roar filling the world, like a fast approaching subway train barreling through its tunnel before entering the station. The purple sky was pin-wheeling to an unfathomable black. His eyelids felt so heavy. He was drifting away...*

*"One day..."*

*It was a man's voice, so close that John felt the other's warm breath against his ear.*

*"You have one day," the man repeated.*

*"Please! Call 911!" John moaned. "I need help!"*

*"One day is all you have," the man insisted.*

*That voice, John recognized it. "Don? Is that you?"*

*"Yes, John. It's me," Donald, his older brother said. He was in his military uniform, like the last time John saw him, just before his deployment to Iraq.*

*"What are you doing here, man?" John said, sitting up.*

*Was he suffering a head injury from being hit by the cab? A concussion? That might explain Don's impossible presence... Even within the peculiar logic of his dream, John knew his brother was dead...*

*Killed in action three years ago, in Baghdad.*

*But here Don was, kneeling in the gutter beside him. John stared deeply into his brother's blue eyes. John could see through Don's military buzz cut that scar across his scalp that John had inflicted back when they were kids, playing sword fights with their sawed off broom sticks and trashcan-lid shields.*

*"Listen to me very carefully, Bro," Don said. "You only have the day to find your purpose and save yourself."*

*"You're not making any sense, Don!"*

*"I'm giving you the greatest gift," Don said." Self awareness."*

*"But one day to figure it all out?" John complained.*

*"That's all the time there is," Don shrugged.*

*John reflexively looked at his watch. The crystal was smashed from the accident. The hands were stopped at 8:02 AM –*

And then he'd woken up, to peer groggily at the drugstore wind-up alarm clock next to the hotplate, by the rusty sink. It had read: 8:02 AM…

Outside, a truck roared past, its vibrations rising up through the creaky floorboards of the attic. Then all was again quiet, except for the ticking of the clock.

John rose from the tattered armchair, where he'd fallen asleep last night after coming home from his bartending job, and crossed to the mirror. The dream had been so vivid that he felt like he had to prove to himself he hadn't been injured by that hit and run cab.

He gazed at his reflection, running his fingers through his long, blond hair. He studied his gaunt features, the lacework of lines around his blue eyes. There wasn't a bruise or abrasion anywhere, of course. It had just been a dream, after all.

Dreaming about being hit by a taxi was freaky enough… the way that cab had hurled him across the pavement like a rag doll… but then to have your dead war hero of a brother show up to issue portends of doom!

"Just what I need," John murmured to his reflection. "To start hearing voices…"

But he hadn't heard voices. Just *one* voice – Don's – and what he'd said so adamantly had been quite *specific*…

That John had only a day to find his purpose and save his life.

Sure, he knew enough pop psychology to understand what was going on. *It all must have to do with my career as an artist,* John thought. *My dream is telling me that I've got to get painting again.*

His easel was in the corner. His paints and brushes were nearby.

But his inspiration was gone – and had been, for quite some time.

The line from an old Cat Stevens song looped in his head, "*... If my colors all run dry...*"

*Wait a minute,* John thought, shuddering. *That song was in my dream, as I lay broken and bleeding in the gutter.*

John, wearing his paint-splattered jeans and a grey, sleeveless sweatshirt with the faded logo of a college from which he'd graduated a lifetime ago, looked at his unsold paintings leaning against the wall and wondered if he would ever paint again.

The attic suddenly felt suffocating. He grabbed his old tan trench coat and hurried out of the apartment, careening down the narrow, switchback flights of stairs to the street.

Outside, he turned up his collar against the rain and walked blindly, hands thrust into his pockets and shoulders hunched against the wet wind.

He was pre-occupied, replaying his grim dream through his mind when he turned the corner at the bodega and almost had his eye put out by an umbrella being carried by a woman.

She looked like the Morton's Salt girl in her tan shorts and yellow rain slicker. He had time to take in her thick auburn hair cascading in curls to her shoulders, and her startled brown eyes... to register how pretty she was.

But then he was past her without so much as excusing himself for bumping into her. When he looked back, she had already gone into the store – probably thinking he was a rude and thoughtless jerk.

John walked and walked. The rain gradually let up and the sun, a pale disk, struggled to break through the wooly gray sky. He walked past the gallery where he'd had his first show, back when he'd imagined that he had a brilliant future as an artist. For a while it had seemed possible. His creativity had blossomed like flowers in spring, the colors brilliant in his mind's eye, the ideas bunching and jostling in boisterous impatience to be first to leap onto the canvas through the ferruled tip of his brush.

But while he sold a painting here and there, he never really broke through to the kind of public notice he'd always dreamed about. The galleries lost interest and John watched like a helpless bystander as his career as an artist spiraled down.

He began displaying his paintings at street festival booths, telling himself the situation was only temporary, and it was, in its own ironic way, because soon he couldn't *afford* the street festival entry fees. Finally he was reduced to propping up his canvases on the sidewalk, with nobody paying the slightest attention except for the cops, who'd gruffly order him to move on.

The sun was growing stronger by the minute, baking away the last of the rain as John found himself approaching the stone embankment of the river that snaked its way through the heart of the city.

He took in the view with his painter's eye and wondered, *where am I in this picture?*

The answer was nowhere. He'd invested his life in his ambition to paint. He had no other interests and no ideas about what he might do with himself now that his ambitious dream had fallen to earth on broken wings.

Well, if his dream last night was truly was an omen, and all he had was this day to discover his true purpose, he was determined to play out the hand life had dealt him, and pass his final moments on earth clutching a paint brush.

# 3. SAVED FROM DROWNING

Annette went walking, too.

After the Bender Construction guys departed, she turned off the burner under the pot of *Nonna* Rita's Sunday gravy, and left the youth center.

The rain had let up and the sun was out. She walked a half-mile to the waterfront, where, if she turned right, she'd be heading towards the ritzy condos and restaurants that were the crown jewels of the ongoing riverfront gentrification being spearheaded by Bender Realty Trust.

Or she could go left, where the waterfront still remained true to the city's ancient history as a port town. There, a succession of bleak warehouses stood with hulking, wooden piers jutting out into the river.

Annette, feeling dour and dismal from her losing battle with Bender, started walking left, away from all the gaudy, bright promise. She was in the mood for somber shadows and the wistful stillness of those vacant, cadaverous buildings past their prime.

She stepped through a gap in the sagging chain link fence guarding an empty warehouse. The fence, festooned with windblown trash, mocked her with its sign: "*Coming Soon – Luxury Waterfront Condos Built by Bender Realty Trust.*"

Shaking her head and muttering to herself, Annette cut across the cracked asphalt yard littered with glass shards, and stepped onto the waterfront pier's wooden planking. Just ahead at the water's edge, there was somebody in the shadows cast by a tall stack of pallets – it looked like a man sitting on an upturned wooden crate. As Annette peered, the figure rose and stepped forward into the sunlight.

He was a small, elderly man with close-cropped silvery hair and whiskers. He wore scuffed, cordovan brogues, threadbare brown corduroy trousers that were baggy at the knees, and a dingy yellow sweater.

A homeless person, Annette thought. There were quite a number of homeless in this part of town. They squatted in the abandoned warehouses.

She abruptly realized that she was quite alone with this guy in this deserted place. Not that he *looked* dangerous… but still…

She was about to turn away and head back to the relative safety of the street, when she saw the guy walk to the pier's very end. Ten feet below him, Annette knew, the deep water eddied and swirled, lapping at the black, oil-slicked pylons, thick as telephone poles.

He was balancing on his heels with the toes of his brogues suspended in mid-air. Then he leaned forward and let himself topple into the river, sending up a terrific splash.

Annette had spent her high school summers working as a lifeguard at the city pool, and now her training took over. She dropped her shoulder bag, shrugged out of the rain slicker, kicked off her flip-flops and sprinted toward the water's edge. She saw the old guy's gray head bobbing in the dark rippling currents as she dove in. The water was cold, but it was more of a relief than a hardship, due to the day's humidity.

"Leave me alone! I want to die!" the old guy whimpered as Annette reached him in just a few powerful scissor-kicks.

He put up a fight, wind-milling his arms, but Annette's lifeguard training continued to hold. She collared him from behind, hooking her arm over his chest and doing a strong, steady sidestroke toward a ladder nailed to the side of the pier.

"Go on, climb up," she scolded, placing the pale, coughing man's hand on the first rung of the ladder.

The man scuttled up the ladder and flopped onto the pier. Annette followed him and then stood, dripping wet, looking down at the guy.

"I told you to I *wanted* to drown," the man whined, unsteadily getting to his feet.

"I think I'd better call the police," Annette said, tucking her wet hair behind her ears. She pretended to reach into her bag for a cell phone – like she could ever afford one.

"No, please don't," the man pleaded. He looked up at the sky. "I guess…" he slowly admitted, "I guess you being here is a sign."

Annette was starting to feel chilled in her wet clothes. "A sign for *what*?"

The man's pale blue eyes began to glisten with tears. "That I need to talk with somebody…"

As the tears rolled down his cheeks, his words came in a rush, as if a dam had burst. "I've been thinking that if I just held on, it would be *all right*, but today I simply decided that I *couldn't go on* all *alone*. I'm so tired of trying to escape the gloom that enfolds me…."

His pain was so palpable that Annette was moved to take his trembling hand. Gazing into his tear streaked face, she told him, "My grandfather always said that when you don't know what to think, just think about God."

"Is your grandfather a devout man?"

"In his way," Annette replied. "He died long ago, and never stepped foot in a church for all the time I knew him. He did tell me once that the Church is *a* place to find God, but it can't be the *only* place, since God is everywhere and made everything."

"Then your grandfather believed God is all around us?"

Annette nodded. "I think he believed that when we're driven by our quest for peace and serenity to reconnect with God, we're really trying to reconnect with life."

"And if you reconnect with life, then you *can't* be alone…" the man said slowly.

"My grandfather also said that a fine way to accomplish that reconnection is to forget about your own troubles by shifting your attention to helping others. He said that you simply can't be gloomy when you're focused on giving another person a helping hand."

"How did your grandfather come to be so wise?" the old man marveled.

"It's a long story," Annette said.

"Well, thank you again for saving me," he said. "You being here to prevent me from making such a terrible mistake was clearly a sign that I must have faith and hold on."

Shivering now in her wet clothes, Annette was grateful for the warmth of her rain slicker as she watched the old man walk away, slipping through the gap in the chain link fence and disappearing down the street.

# 4. BALLOONS IN THE PARK

In the past, John's best work had been the garden landscapes he'd painted at City Park. Back at his apartment, he threw on fresh, if equally paint-stained chinos and a faded, red and black plaid flannel shirt. He folded up his easel, packed his art supplies into a canvas bag, hauled everything downstairs to his ancient Toyota pickup parked in the back alley, and drove over to City Park.

Being a weekday, he easily found a space in the lot. He shouldered his easel and canvas bag, and trudged through the park's tall, wrought iron front gates, following the winding cobblestone path to his favorite spot by the gardens, near the great bronze fountain that sent skywards a shimmering spray.

It had become a truly beautiful day, sunny and warm. The air was filled with the scent of cotton candy and the cheerful music coming from the merry-go-round across the way. The park was filled with young mothers pushing strollers, and older folks who sunned themselves on the rows of dark green benches bordering the paths.

Nearby, a middle-aged woman stood next to her small wooden pushcart filled with boxes of Cracker Jack, chocolate bars and other snacks. Tied to the pushcart was a bouquet of candy-colored balloons, vibrant as giant lollipops and luminous against the dark lattice of trees.

John set up his easel and waited for inspiration to come.

And waited. And waited.

He gazed at the gardens. With the sun steadily rising in the sky he was excruciatingly aware of time ticking away.

Driving over he'd been adrenalized by his dream, certain that this would be the day that he would paint his masterpiece and come to be recognized as a great artist, because surely *that* was his purpose in life?

*That* was what was expected by the admonishing voice inside him, represented in his dream by his dead brother?

But now that the moment of truth had arrived, he found his imagination as blank as the canvas before him.

Where was Don now that John needed him? He could use some inspiration – no matter how macabre the muse…

He looked again at the balloon peddler lady and a long forgotten memory rose up: *Mom and Dad bringing Don and me to this very spot when we were little and buying us balloons from a man who sold them exactly where that lady's cart is now. I would always get a blue one. Don a red one. And try as we might – knowing we would be so sad about it later – we couldn't resist letting our balloons go, so we could watch them race together high into the sky, and wonder whose balloon would first get to heaven…*

John tried to swallow away the sudden lump in his throat.

*I guess you get the last laugh, Don. You beat me, after all…*

As if of its own volition his hand began a pencil sketch of the woman at her pushcart, adding in a lamppost and shrubs for background. And then, blinking back tears, he sketched into the foreground a happy couple and their two young sons. Each boy was reaching for a balloon as their parents' hands rested on their shoulders.

John exchanged his pencil for a fan-head brush and slashed a bold swath of cobalt across the canvas to create an expanse of sky...

Intent on his painting, John looked up for the first time when a distant church bell chimed two o'clock, and saw the woman trundling her little pushcart in his direction. She wore a light blue sleeveless blouse, loose-fitting green denim overalls and black sneakers. Now that she was closer, she looked to be in her sixties, with wings of steel gray hair poking out from beneath her orange baseball cap.

"I take it you were painting me?" the woman asked. When John nodded, she continued, "May I see?"

"Sure," John said. He watched her as she gazed at his work.

"You made up the family buying the balloons," the woman murmured. "I had no such customers today."

"That's my folks and my brother and me, from a long time ago," John explained. "We used to come here on Saturdays and we bought balloons from a guy who had your spot."

The woman's face softened. "That was my husband, Anthony, you bought your balloons from!" she exclaimed. "May God rest his soul," she added.

"I remember him as being a nice man," John offered.

"Oh, he was a lovely man," the woman agreed.

"So now you sell balloons to make a living?" John asked.

"A living?" the woman chuckled. "My Anthony was a bus driver for the city for 30 years. He left me a pension so I make ends meet. He only sold from the cart on weekends, for a hobby. He loved to see the children smile. Now *I* do it."

"Why?" John asked, mystified, thinking there'd be better ways for this woman to spend her time.

"Well, you'd probably think me silly, but when I push this little cart that he used to push and do what he loved to do, I feel like I'm close to him."

"Wow, I didn't think of it that way," John said, moved by the woman's story. "I guess that's why I come to this spot, as well. It makes me feel like I'm close to my family."

"They're gone like my Anthony?"

"Yeah…" he said simply, and nothing more.

Long ago he'd locked away the painful details of his family's demise in the deepest corner of his heart. He would not reopen the wounds by dredging up the sorry tale.

"Well, I think that's a nice painting," the woman said.

"Thank you."

"It's no masterpiece," she hedged.

"No, of course not," John said dryly.

"But it's a happy painting," she offered.

"Yeah," John murmured, "I guess it is. A loving family, happy in the moment…"

The woman nodded, and stuck out her hand. "My name's Marie."

"I'm John," he said, shaking hands.

That's quite a nice collection of brushes you have there," Marie observed.

"They're old, but serviceable."

"Hogs bristle?" Marie asked.

"You know brushes?" John asked, surprised.

"I know a bit… That shape is called a 'round,'" she said pointing. "That one's a 'flat' and that one is a 'filbert'…"

"Very good," John said.

"Say, do you mind if I try my hand at painting?" she asked. Before John knew it, she'd picked up his palette and most tapered brush, and dipped it into the black pigment. "I'll work fast," she promised as she shouldered him aside and commandeered his easel.

John, figuring it was easier to humor her, removed his painting from the easel, replacing it with his remaining blank canvas. "You might want to sketch something first."

"Not necessary," Marie announced.

John, shrugging, sat down on a nearby bench.

"Thank you so much for letting me do this, John."

"I'm glad you're enjoying yourself, but it's no big deal."

"That's not true!" Marie admonished. "You're *giving* a great deal."

"What? My time?"

"In part. And you're giving me the use of your art supplies, right?"

"What? Five bucks worth of paint and canvas? That's nothing." John pointed to the massive bronze fountain. "The guy who paid for *that* gave a lot."

"The guy who paid for that, probably just wrote a check," Marie countered. "When it comes to charity, what matters isn't the size of the gift, but the manner in which it's given." She paused. "Have you ever heard the story of the 'widow's coins'?"

"No."

"It's a story from the Bible about how Jesus watched the rich cast their gifts into the Temple basket," she began. "The rich men all put in bulging sacks of gold, of course. Then Jesus saw a poor widow put in just two meager coins, which was all she had. Jesus then said to his

Disciples, '*Truly, I say to you that this poor widow has cast in more than all the others…*'"

"I think I understand," John said. "She gave everything she had, while those rich guys weren't going to miss their donations."

Marie nodded. "Jesus understood that it is the *intention* of the charitable gift, far more than its *size*, that counts."

"I still don't think I did that much… Like I said, just five bucks worth of paint and canvas…"

"Like the widow's coins, they're worth everything to *you*," Marie countered, her brown eyes beaming. "That makes it the greatest act of charity possible. Five bucks worth of charity like that will someday save the world, John, you just wait and see."

"Yes, ma'am" John said politely, thinking, *crazy, old loon…* He hadn't given his minor act of charity any thought at all, being distracted by his own gloom.

There! I'm finished!" Marie set down the brush.

John, skeptical, at what she could have accomplished in so short a time, stepped around the easel – and stared transfixed.

Onto the canvas she'd traced in bold, graceful, black strokes a series of calligraphic characters almost three dimensional in their elegant beauty.

"That's calligraphy," John said. "You weren't painting, you were *writing*."

"Calligraphy *is* painting," Marie said. "How we paint the words provides the meaning."

It's Chinese?" John asked in wonderment.

"Japanese," Marie said.

"How do you know how to do this?"

"My father taught me."

"Your father was Japanese?

"No, silly! Italian."

"I don't get it..."

"It's a long story."

"Okay," John chuckled, shaking his head. "Well, what does it say?"

"It's an apology," Marie said. "To my daughter."

As she reached for her painting, John said, "It's still wet, be careful."

"I will. You know, with my wet painting and my balloon cart, it's quite a lot for me. You have a lot of stuff, too, I see. You don't by any chance have a truck?"

"It just so happens I do." John folded up his easel and stowed the rest of his supplies in his canvas bag.

"How about a lift?"

"Now you want a ride?" He tried to sound aggrieved but his heart wasn't in it. The incredible goofiness of this situation seemed to loosen him up. He suddenly felt light-hearted in a way he hadn't felt in a long time, as Marie's story about the 'widow's coins' reverberated within his mind and heart...

All he'd ever wanted to do through his painting was touch other people... that was how art was immortal, wasn't it? He'd always dreamed of a day when people around the world – people he would never know – would view his work and be moved to joy or wistful contemplation, and for that brief instant his soul and theirs would be merged.

And so, if he'd managed today to touch at least one person – Marie – maybe that was his dream coming true in its own way. It was certainly a *start…*

"Tell you what," John said. "I'll trade you a ride for two balloons."

"Take your pick," Marie said.

John chose a red one and a blue one, and then released them.

*For you, Don…*

John watched the balloons drift, dwindling, until they were just red and blue dots against the pale denim sky, like daubs of paint on his canvas. Then vanished.

*Gone to heaven.*

# 5. MORTON'S SALT GIRL

John took the lead as they left the park, carrying his art stuff while Marie trundled behind, pushing her cart with its tether of balloons bobbing in the breeze. At the truck, John loaded in his painting supplies and then maneuvered the cart into the flatbed.

The woman was quiet during the short drive. "Turn in here!" she abruptly said.

John did, came to a stop and shut off the truck. "I've walked by this place a thousand times," he said. "The city youth center."

It was a long, low, flat-roofed building set back on an asphalt lot, delineated on one side by a chain link fence and on the other by a tall, cinderblock wall. As John exited his truck he noticed a group of tough-looking, Black teenagers who had been hanging out by the wall, staring at him.

He looked around and saw that the opposite corners of the yard were taken up with mixed gender groups of Latino and Asian teens. The three gangs had staked out their turf in the yard. Acutely aware of being the gangs' new focus of attention, he wrestled the old woman's cart out of the truck.

"You bring my cart inside so it doesn't get stolen," Marie demanded. "Just push it over the front step and then I'll take it."

John did as he was told as she held the door open for him to push the cart inside. The balloons scraped the low ceiling of the front hallway, its dingy walls painted pale green. John wedged it into a corner and then turned to go.

"Who's there?" a woman called out.

"It's me, Annette!" Marie replied.

"Mom?" The woman appeared in the doorway.

*It's the Morton's Salt girl I bumped into by the bodega this morning,* John realized.

Now that he had a good look at her he saw she was even more beautiful than he'd first surmised.

This morning she'd been wearing shorts, but now she was dressed in faded jeans, an emerald green cotton sweater and moccasins. Her shoulder length, thick dark hair looked damp, like she was fresh from the shower.

"Mom? Who is this?" She studied John with just the hint of a smile playing at the corners of her wide mouth and sparkling in her big, brown eyes. "You look very familiar."

"A painter from the gardens in the park, near my corner," the old woman explained. "He helped me with my cart."

"My name's John." He paused. "My God, what are you cooking? I've never smelled anything so delicious!"

"That's my *madre* Rita's Special Sunday Gravy," Marie boasted. "Annette, why are you making that now?"

"It's a long story, Mom. Thank you for helping my mother," she smiled at John. "It almost makes up for ramming into me this morning and not stopping to apologize."

"Oh, you recognized me..."

"You're too handsome to forget," Annette said.

I'm really sorry about that," John stammered, embarrassed. "It was very rude of me, I was distracted, but that's no excuse I know..."

It dawned on him what she'd just said. "Wait! I'm too *what*?"

"Forget it – bumping into me, that is," she teased. "I'm Annette. I'm really pleased to meet you, and to see you're not some crazy weirdo."

"I'm not a weirdo, at least," John chuckled. "Anyway, you run this place?"

"Yes," she replied.

"With those gangs out there?" John frowned. "That could be dangerous."

"That's what I tell her," Marie interjected. "She works here all alone. I understand she is trying to do good, but I worry about her here all alone."

Mom..." Annette rolled her eyes. "Let's not argue again."

"Okay!" Marie held up her hands in surrender. "No more fighting. Look, I made you an apology." She reached into the cart for the calligraphic canvas and handed it to her daughter.

Annette studied it. "Thank you, Mama," she said. "I'm going to hang it in my office. I love you."

"I love you, too," Marie said.

"What does it say?" John asked.

"Basically it says she understands why I do this work, and that my father, if he were alive, would be proud."

She moved closer to John so he could see the canvas. "See these characters?"

平 和

Her slender fingers traced lightly over the still damp canvas...

# 調和

John noticed she didn't wear wedding or engagement rings…

# 啓発

"They represent from top to bottom, *peace, harmony and enlightenment*," Annette explained.

John felt her standing so close. Their shoulders were touching. She smelled like flowers. He became weak-kneed and dizzy as the world began to swirl. To think that she had been just around the corner of his life all this time… He wished he could make this wonderful moment last forever.

Don's words from the dream came back hauntingly…

*One day, that's all there is…*

*A profound epiphany seemed maddeningly poised on the verge of John's realization, like a word can get stuck on the tip of your tongue. Don loomed large in his mind's eye. His brother's expression was watchful, expectant…*

*What do I know that I've forgotten? John wondered. What is Don trying to tell me?*

*John tried to comprehend what was so tantalizingly in front of him, the way he did when he looked at the world to visualize the composition of a painting… to see with his artist's eye…*

Then the floor seemed to steady beneath him. The sense that he was tottering on the precipice of a great realization faded. John felt unaccountably sad, like a child on a carousel who'd missed his chance at the brass ring as the ride slows to its end.

"– My mother wrote that she's really proud of me for trying to bring a measure of peace, harmony and enlightenment into the world," Annette was saying.

"Even if she does spend her whole life here," Marie complained. "And makes so many personal sacrifices for those kids."

Annette smiled. "Mom, you know we're to sacrifice ourselves in order to attain the salvation of others."

"Don't quote Dharma to me, little girl," Marie scolded.

"'Dharma?'" John repeated. "Are you Buddhists?"

"We're Italian-Americans," Marie said proudly.

"So then how *do* you both know how to write and read Japanese calligraphy, and all about Dharma, for that matter?" John asked.

"My grandfather learned about it in World War Two. He taught my mother, and she taught me," Annette said.

"Your grandfather? I don't get it," John said.

"It's a long story," Annette smiled. "But if you'd like to hear it?"

"Sure," John said, thinking, *I could listen to you forever.*

"My grandfather was Hector LaFlame," Annette began. "They called him 'Slingshot LaFlame.' He was a pitcher for the Boston Red Sox for a couple of years, until he suffered a career-ending shoulder injury…"

## 6. RED SOX 1 — SENJINKUN 0

It was 1944 in the Pacific, and the Japanese were on the run.

Maybe that's why U.S. Army Air Force Lieutenant Hector LaFlame and his wingman, Lieutenant Danny Silver, were a bit too complacent when they veered off their flight plan during their routine patrol off the Solomon Islands.

And perhaps why the two seasoned fighter pilots didn't see the hornet swarm of Jap Zeros that dove upon them from out of the sun – until it was too late.

Before Hector even knew what was happening, Danny was gone, vanished in a ball of orange fire and black smoke as his P-47 Thunderbolt "Jug" was pelted with a storm of Jap machine gun fire.

Hector's feet danced on the rudder pedals as he jammed the stick between his knees hard to starboard, putting his Jug into a sharp bank to escape the enemy strafing. He thought he was going to make it, but then he heard the clack and rattle of bullets pelting his plane. Jap tracer rounds must have hit the Jug's control lines. The stick went dead and his state-of-the-art fighter was reduced to a plummeting brick.

*Time to go*, Hector thought as his plane began its swan song toward the beckoning blue and emerald waters of the Pacific. He shoved back the canopy and bailed.

Shrieking wind filled his ears as he tumbled toward the water 3,000 feet below. It took every ounce of his willpower to not immediately pull the ripcord, but he knew he had to wait until the last possible moment. The Jap fighter jockeys had a nasty habit of using Allied pilots for target practice as they dangled helplessly beneath their chutes.

When he couldn't delay any longer he pulled the cord. As his silk deployed he endured the neck snapping halt to his freefall, and began gently swinging like a pendulum beneath the open canopy. He glimpsed his beloved, silver fighter plane, leaking black smoke and orange flames, plow into the blue-green sea.

Then Hector looked down between the tops of his boots at the ocean rising up fast. He squeezed shut his eyes and braced for impact…

*And his life passed before him, as viewed from a succession of pitcher's mounds in ballparks across America, his fingers wrapped around the curved hide of a baseball like the natural extension of his arm…*

They told him at the orphanage in Philadelphia that he came over from Italy when he was just an infant, back around 1920. He didn't remember his parents, who both died before his first birthday, and he never knew what his real name was – he guessed it was some version of the Hector LaFlame moniker they'd stuck him with at Ellis Island.

Growing up in Philly, he'd been a washout in school, but he'd always been an excellent athlete – especially at baseball. For as long as he could remember he'd been able to pitch. Curveball… slider… changeup… knuckleball… and his own blazing fastball – his 'slingshot' throw for which he'd been dubbed with his nickname of Slingshot LaFlame.

He dropped out of high school at seventeen and started playing the Eastern Seaboard semipro circuit. Two years later, Hector was down south in the Minors, where a scout saw him and got him a try out with the Boston Red Sox, who signed him. He was a little intimidated by it all his first year, but he blossomed in 1939, with a 22-win season, and seven shutouts.

Everything was coming up roses until that home game at Fenway against the Washington Senators, on April 24, 1940.

Hector was on the mound at the top of the ninth.

The score was 7–8, Senators.

The bases were loaded.

Bucky Jacobs was at bat.

The count was 2 balls – 2 strikes.

Fenway was hushed as Hector leaned toward home plate to take the sign from his catcher, Johnny Peacock. Of course, he already knew what Peacock was going to signal: Hector had to retire Jacobs if the Sox were to have a chance…

It was time to unleash the 'slingshot.'

*He wound up with every fiber of his being focused on the task. But as his arm snapped forward he felt an excruciating fire ignite deep within his shoulder. He cried out like he'd been shot. The baseball fell lifeless from his trembling fingers to roll a few inches down the incline of the mound and then stop – forever.*

He was crying like a baby, cradling his suddenly useless arm as they escorted him off the field. He should have been embarrassed at the scene he was making, but his shoulder hurt too much for him to care.

When the docs took a look they said he ripped his *whoos'is* and had chips in his *what'sis*... Hector stopped listening to the ten-dollar words when the docs said they couldn't make him whole again.

His baseball career was over. His dream had burst like a balloon, just when he'd managed to breathe life into it.

His shoulder eventually healed up enough for ordinary work, but with his pitching wing clipped, he had no skills. He tried to make a go of it with a series of dead end jobs on loading docks and factory floors, but it hurt too damn much to overhear the talk of others about who that scowling, shambling day laborer *used* to be.

He was alone, angry, bitter. He felt murderous violence simmering within, and figured if he was going to kill somebody – *anybody* – he ought to join the Army, and do it with government approval. At boot camp he set his sights on being an Army fighter pilot, and of course he did swell. He still had his superb athletic coordination... his hawk-sharp eyesight and his grace under pressure. He just couldn't pitch anymore and he was mad as hell about it.

You might say he had a chip *on* his shoulder as well as chips *within* it.

In 1942, after Pearl Harbor, the Army Air Corps was renamed the Army Air Force, and as one of the AAF's lieutenant fighter pilots, Hector found himself with a few million other of his closest friends in various shades of khaki in the Pacific Theater. He flew over 40 missions and shot down four Jap planes. One more and he'd be an ace.

But then he hit a dry patch. He went mission after mission with no kills. Pro ball was gone from his life but he still cared about *winning*, and he was feeling like he was in the closing innings of his opportunity to bag his fifth Jap bird and finish up the war as an ace.

Hector's natural and hugely fierce sense of competition kicked in – it was the same driving instinct to win that had taken him to the major leagues. So today he'd bullied his wingman Danny Silver to abandon their flight plan and hunt in new territory in the hopes of bagging his fifth bird with those big red 'meatballs' on its wings and fuselage…

But instead, *they'd* gotten bagged…

Good old Danny was now smoke and ash…

Hector was dangling from his chute…

*The water was rushing up at him and –*

He hit the water hard, the impact jarring his pistol from out of his shoulder holster as he went under about ten feet, and then struggled and kicked his way to the surface with the buoyant aid of his canary yellow Mae West vest. Sputtering, he shrugged out of his chute harness and began to dog paddle toward a nearby island.

By the time he dragged himself up on the shell strewn, rocky beach he was exhausted, so he didn't have much in him when he saw the lone Jap soldier staring at him from twenty feet away. He was a short, middle-aged looking guy. He was barefoot, in a ragged tan, Imperial Army uniform. He had no gun but he was holding a shiny samurai sword.

"Stay back!" Hector yelled. His right hand slapped longingly at his empty shoulder holster. He had a folding knife in his pocket, but its three-inch blade didn't seem like much of a match for that Japanese saber.

"Stay back!" Hector repeated as Tojo approached. *Or I'll yell 'stay back again,'* Hector thought helplessly.

The Jap was peering at him. *Probably measuring me for a haircut at shoulder level with that damned sword of his*, Hector worried.

Then Hector's right hand closed around a baseball sized rock pressing against his heaving belly, and he knew *he* was going to be the one to walk away from this tussle.

*I don't have my fastball anymore*, Hector thought. *But I still got enough of an arm to tag that Nip right between his slant-eyes, and split his skull.*

The image of inflicting violence on another, and thus chiseling away at the dark and dismal universe that had robbed him of his heartfelt dreams, revitalized him in both body and spirit. Hector quickly rose to his feet and wound up, about to hurl the rock and knock Tojo's block off.

But what the Jap did next changed both their lives forever.

The Jap said in perfect English, "Slingshot? Is that you?"

Hector warily lowered his arm. "How do you know me?"

The Jap was now grinning. "I saw you pitch a no-hitter against Cleveland at Fenway in 1939, when I was a graduate student at Harvard."

# #

"My name is Kanbun Daishi," the Jap told Hector. "Captain Kanbun Daishi."

They were sitting on driftwood, beside the flat stone hearth that took up the center of Captain Daishi's campsite. The site was hidden from view of Allied air patrols by the verdant fronds of tall coconut palms, and from the sea patrols by high dunes. The camp had a thatch-roof hut woven from rattan. Beside the hut was a large wooden crate. Surrounding the little campsite, hanging from every nearby jungle vine and branch, were strips of parchment intricately covered with Jap writing.

"My name doesn't mean anything to you," Daishi began, "But it is quite significant in my own country. You see, I am a direct descendant of Kōbō Daishi, one of the greatest geniuses Japan has ever produced."

Daishi had given Hector fresh water in a hollowed out coconut shell – it turned out the island was blessed with a spring fed by rainwater – and was expertly using his sword to carve thin slices of raw fish, which he then fanned out on a plate carved from tree bark.

"You're pretty good with that samurai sword, Captain Daishi," Hector ventured.

"Please, call me Kanbun. And this is not a samurai sword. It's called a '*katana*.' It is standard issue to officers."

"Well, you're still right handy with it."

Hector frowned as Kanbun offered him the plate of raw fish. "Don't suppose you could slap a few of those fillets on the fire for me?"

"Of course, Slingshot," Kanbun said politely. He placed chunks of fish on the hot stone and within a few moments Hector was hungrily devouring the freshest most succulent seafood since Bobby Doerr had taken him out to dinner at Boston's Union Oyster House, back in '39.

"So you were talking about your, uh, *honorable ancestors*," Hector said between bites, trying to be polite, still not convinced this all wasn't some Jap ruse, and that Kanbun wasn't going to grab up his sword and take a swing at him, the way Ted Williams swung his trusty bat when he was blasting the ball out of Fenway.

"My great, great, great grandfather Kōbō Daishi was many things – a scholar, poet, artist, calligrapher, and the founder of *Shingon*

Buddhism in Japan – but he was never a samurai, a warrior," Kanbun said. "Quite the contrary, Slingshot. As one of my country's most renowned Buddhist masters, he devoted his life to spreading the divine *Shingon* message that all have the seeds of the Buddha within, and that with practice, anyone can achieve enlightenment in this lifetime."

"Not like you, huh?" Hector said. "You being an Army captain and all."

"Alas, I was drafted," Kanbun said. "After my graduate studies in linguistics at Harvard – where I was an avid follower of your career so tragically cut short, and the Red Sox, I might add – I was a professor at Tokyo University. I managed to use my family connections to avoid most of the war, but I was finally drafted. Due to my illustrious ancestry and my professional status, I was given my captain's commission. I was on a troop carrier with my men when we were attacked from the sky. Our ship sank and I found myself in the water. I climbed upon that large wooden crate, the one you that you see there beside my hut. I floated for days, until I washed ashore here."

"How long have you been here?" Hector asked.

"Six months," Kanbun replied.

"What!" Hector was astonished. "Good God, man! There's allied air and sea patrols that pass hereabouts. Why didn't you light a signal fire to be rescued?"

"Slingshot, I have no wish to be a prisoner of war, assuming I would even be allowed to live long enough to assume that status," Kanbun said. "Not when I have everything I could want right here: plenty of fish, fresh water, and the solitude to meditate and strive to follow my great ancestor, Kōbō Daishi's path to enlightenment through the meditation of calligraphy. Did I mention he *invented* modern calligraphy?"

"You might have, and I wasn't paying attention," Hector mumbled around a mouth full of fish.

Kanbun gestured toward the parchments softly rustling in the breeze. "Every day I focus on my calligraphy, intent on every brush stroke, and in this way I move closer to being at one with the universe."

"Where'd you *get* all this paper, and your pens and inks, and what not?" Hector asked.

Kanbun smiled. "It is the most wondrous thing, Hector, almost as if this were all meant to be –"

Kanbun's sweeping gesture seemed to take in the white fillets of fish sizzling on the gray rock, the orange flicker of the fire, the rustle of the ivory parchments hanging from the tawny vines, the rumble of turquoise breakers on the tan beach, the green palms, and the vast canopy of deep blue sky –

And Kanbun's gesture also encompassed Hector, who couldn't quite believe that this wasn't all a dream, him sitting here eating grilled fish and chatting away with a Japanese Army captain.

"You see, Slingshot, in that crate that saved my life, that I floated upon to this very island, were ample calligraphy supplies which were to me more valuable than gold."

"But you've got all your writings outside," Hector said. "It rains in these parts every day. Doesn't it all get washed away just as soon as you're done?"

Kanbun smiled.

*Crazy Jap*, Hector thought. "Can I ask you another question?"

"We have the time, Slingshot."

"When you first saw me on the beach, you were carrying your sword… Were you planning on doing me in? I mean, before you recognized me, that is?"

"Absolutely not," Kanbun declared, surprisingly seemingly affronted that Hector might have thought so ill of him. "I had my *katana* because I always have it with me, merely as a *tool* – in case I come upon something useful on the beach. I have never in my life harmed another human being and I had no intention of doing so – despite *Senjinkun*."

"What's uh, what you just said?"

"*Senjinkun* is the field service code of martial honor that Army Minister Hideki wrote to guide members of the Imperial Armed Forces. It states that we must show no mercy to the enemy and not allow ourselves to be prisoners."

"But you don't believe in it?"

"No. I follow the code of *kanzen chōaku*."

"What's *that*?" Hector asked, even more bewildered.

"It's a rather complex system of ethical principals," Kanbun smiled. "But essentially, it can be distilled down to the concept of something called karma. In my culture, karma is very much like your Golden Rule."

"'*Do onto others as you would have them do onto you*,'" Hector nodded.

"Precisely," Kanbun said. "It is especially meaningful to me because among my ancestor Kōbō Daishi's many accomplishments, he is also the patron saint of pilgrims traveling in search of enlightenment. There is in my culture a strong tradition of giving charity to such pilgrims." Kanbun paused. "Pilgrims like *you*, for instance."

"*Me*?" Hector blurted, astonished. "*I'm* no pilgrim searching for nothing…"

Kanbun studied him. "Aren't you?"

# #

For a week, Hector and Kanbun spent their days fishing, and gathering firewood and coconuts. Kanbun also began to teach Hector the art of calligraphy as a way of spiritual meditation.

In turn, Hector regaled Kanbun – who was a veritable fountain of baseball stats in general and Red Sox lore specifically – with anecdotes about his time in the major leagues, and what players like Ted Williams, Bobby Doerr, Moe Berg, Johnny Peacock and Doc Cramer were really like.

On their eighth day together, they were on the beach, gathering driftwood for the fire, when Hector's keen eyes spotted a glinting speck coming their way in the clear blue sky.

As it got closer, he recognized the unique gull-wing silhouette of a U.S. Marines Corsair fighter.

All Hector had to do was stay where he was on the beach and the Marine pilot was sure to spot him…

Hector thought about the week that had just passed. The peace he had begun to feel living each simple day moment by moment, as Kanbun had instructed him.

He was progressing nicely in his calligraphy as part of his daily meditation on a riddle that Kanbun had shared with him. He called it a 'koan,' and it went:

*What is the most precious thing in the world?*

*A dead cat, because no one can name it's price...*

Kanbun had shown Hector how to write the riddle in Japanese characters. Every day, Hector banished all the dark and gloom inside of him for the space of time it took to concentrate on carefully tracing the symbols, by turns graceful and slashing, onto a strip of parchment.

When finished, he hung his parchment to rustle softly in the breeze. And every day, the afternoon rains washed the ink away...

During these rain showers, Kanbun would retreat to the hut, but Hector would remain outside, surrendering himself to the torrents so cleansing and renewing. He'd watch as the rain soaked through the strips of parchment, melting the painstakingly drawn characters into inky rivulets, and ultimately, inevitably, into nothingness.

And in the rain, Hector thought about how a person's hopes and dreams – realized or not – were kind of like those symbols he daubed in ink, or his footprints on the beach... just waiting to be washed away by a sudden and uncontrollable deluge...

Or an enemy fighter diving on you from out of the sun...

Or bone chips in your shoulder...

And it came to him that the only thing constant in life was its exquisite and heartbreaking impermanence...

And something momentous seemed on the very verge of revealing itself to Hector...

...Except that the U.S. Marine Corsair fighter was closing on them quickly now.

Rescue was imminent.

But what Hector did next changed both men's lives forever.

He looked at Kanbun and asked, "Do you want to be rescued?"

"Slingshot," Kanbun said softly. "For me, rescue will mean spending the rest of the war in a POW camp."

"Bad karma," Hector declared. "Let's hide!"

# #

Under Kanbun's tutelage, Hector continued his spiritual pilgrimage on the island for almost a year. With Kanbun's subtle and cryptic nudging, Hector learned to see the world as it really *was*, not how it *looked*... and how if Hector's relentless spirit of competition compelled him to *win* at life, that meant he had to *surrender* to life... which was really the *only way* to beat life at its own damned game...

*What is the most precious thing in the world?*

*A dead cat, because no one can name its price...*

The koan didn't ever exactly make sense to Hector in his *head*, but it came to feel everlastingly true in his *heart*...

Hector's spiritual sojourn might have continued even longer, but Kanbun suffered an injury – a serious cut to his leg while hacking brush with his *katana*. Hector, concerned that the wound might become infected and life threatening – *totally and overwhelmingly focused on the wellbeing of his friend* – knew the jig was up.

Soon an Allied plane flew overhead and Hector walked out on the open beach, waving his arms.

The pilot waggled his wings to show Hector that he'd been seen.

"I have a gift for you," Kanbun announced as the two men waited for the rescue ship to arrive. "Something to remember me by."

"I could never forget you," Hector said, embracing his friend.

"Nevertheless, I want you to have it."

Kanbun unbuttoned the breast pocket of his ragged tunic and took from it a wadded piece of paper, greenish in tint. As Kanbun carefully unfolded it, Hector saw that it was a United States five-dollar bill.

"I won it in a game of chance from another officer while on the troop carrier," Kanbun explained.

"Don't you want to keep it?" Hector asked. "You might need the money."

"Slingshot, in a short while I shall be a prisoner of war," Kanbun replied patiently. "It would be taken from me. Besides, that officer I won it from was a combat veteran. He said he took it from the body of an American soldier. Giving it to you will change the bill's karma."

Hector nodded. "I'll keep it always. Thank you."

"It is *I* who thank *you*," Kanbun said and bowed to Hector, something he had never done before. "I am grateful for having been blessed with the opportunity to emulate my illustrious ancestor, Kōbō Daishi, by giving charity to a holy pilgrim in search of enlightenment."

"I don't understand how I helped you," Hector said.

"Slingshot, I am so filled with joy to have spent this time with you, watching firsthand how you have blossomed through my teaching…" Kanbun's voice broke and a tear rolled down his cheek.

Hector stared at his friend and mentor, transfixed. He had seen many different aspects of Kanbun, but never had he seen the man so choked with deeply felt emotion.

"You see, Slingshot, while you were meditating on your calligraphy, I have meditated upon *you*… You are the achievement of my life, and have become my brother…my son… my *legacy*. What I have poured into you from my heart and soul, you will now, in turn, pour into others, long after I am gone. My profound influence upon you has brought me equally profound peace and contentment."

Kanbun smiled. "I wonder now if when I watched you from the bleachers at Fenway so many years and worlds ago, if some part of me knew that one day our karmas would intersect and we would change each other's lives." He shrugged. "The divine symmetry of it all makes me weep, but with tears of joy, because now I feel at last worthy to take my place beside Kōbō Daishi!"

When the Navy rescue party arrived, Hector told them, "This man needs medical attention! Please treat him kindly! He saved my life!" *In more ways than you can ever know*, Hector added to himself.

The sailors looked at their prisoner with sudden respect – tales of Japanese treating Allied personnel with decency were quite the novelty.

"Don't worry, Lieutenant," a sailor replied. "We'll take good care of him until we can ship him home. Guess you fellows couldn't know, but the war's been over for months."

The sailor's words were a clap of thunder reverberating in Hector. The last flimsy veils fell from his eyes and the world stripped of illusion, flooded in, filling him to the brim of his mind, body and spirit.

*My* war is over, *too*, Hector realized. I'm at *peace*.

# 7. CHARITABLE LIFELINE

"And that's how my grandfather learned calligraphy," Annette told John. "He taught it to my mother when she was a little girl, and she eventually taught it to me."

"What happened to your grandfather after the war?" John asked.

"He opened a diner here in the neighborhood. One day a woman came in looking for a waitressing job. Her name was Rita. It wasn't long before they were married. *Nonno* always used to say that if it hadn't been for Kanbun, he never would have had the eyes to see her."

"Did your grandfather ever see Kanbun again?"

Annette nodded. "When I was around fifteen, he came to visit. He was quite old and physically frail, but his mind was still sharp as a tack. He was an important scholar and writer in Japan, I remember... And I'll never forget the power of his spiritual presence."

"But you never became a Buddhist," John asked.

"No," Annette said. "I just try through my work to uphold the Bodhisattva ideal of giving by devoting oneself to the liberation of others from suffering," she added. "Like those kids out there in the yard, for instance. They're pilgrims on a path, just like my *nonno*, Hector. Their lives are stunted with suspicion, bigotry and fear. If I can help mitigate the needless suffering of just one kid due to his intolerance, I'll have done quite a lot in the world, don't you think?"

"How can changing the attitude of just one kid make a difference?"

John shook his head. "I mean, there's so much hatred in the world…"

Annette smiled. "Just because I can't solve *all* the world's problems doesn't mean I can't solve *some* of them. More to the point, not being able to fix *everything* doesn't absolve me of the moral obligation to fix what I *can*."

She took John's hand. "Your lifeline runs across your palm, right? It's supposed to represent your physical vitality. In a similar way, I think that crease across your palm also symbolizes your *Charitable Lifeline*. It represents our spiritual vitality and the state of our connectivity to the world."

John forced himself to focus on what she was saying. It felt really nice to have her holding his hand.

"Everybody knows that being connected to others is a good thing when it comes to work and social life," Annette continued. "Connectivity is paramount in one's spiritual life as well. Your Charitable Lifeline runs like this…"

From left to right on John's palm, Annette tapped the progression:

**"Generosity  →  Giving  →  Positive action  →  Gratitude  → Satisfaction"**

"I think I get it," John said. "I get myself in a mindset where I feel **generous**… then I **give**. Maybe I give money or of myself in some way, like volunteering. Next, I get an emotional charge from taking a **positive action**. And when I receive the gratitude of whoever it was I helped, I feel **satisfaction**, the way Kanbun felt gratified to firsthand witness the transformation his act of giving brought about for your grandfather, Hector."

"That's right," Annette said. "Those steps along the Charitable Lifeline get you *connected* to yourself, to the person you helped, and to the world – provided you invest yourself by savoring the experience and paying full attention to your giving." She released John's hand, much to his sorrow. "You can travel the path of the Charitable Lifeline and experience its benefits by involving yourself in any charity you choose, whether it benefits people close to home or those halfway around the world… *All it takes is being fully aware and attentive during your moments of giving.*"

"I guess for me the hard part is to feel generous in the first place," John mused. "I get kind of wrapped up in my own problems. It makes me feel dark about life in general and not really sympathetic to the problems of others."

"We all feel that way from time to time," Annette reassured him. "It's just being human, but so is our natural tendency to be generous. What can help ratchet up your impulse to be generous is visualizing the recipient of your generosity."

"You're losing me again," John said.

"Let me put it another way," Annette said. "The level of generosity we feel toward somebody is dictated by the familiarity we have with that person."

"That makes sense," John said. "But what if we *don't* personally know the individual who needs our generosity?"

"That's where a proper perspective and mindset play their part," Annette replied. "We can make it our practice to think of *everyone in the world as someone we know…*"

John nodded. "So if I *pretend* I know somebody in Africa who is starving, I'll feel more generous and send money to an organization to help feed that person – is that what you're getting at?"

"Two things," Annette said. "First, I don't happen to believe it's a matter of *pretending* – I think we're *all* part of the family of man, so in a spiritual sense, I really *do know* that starving person in Africa."

"Okay," John acknowledged.

"Second, the end goal isn't to *feel generous*. The end goal is to feel the high that comes from being charitable. You get that simply by being completely invested in terms of attention to each step along the Charitable Lifeline."

"It's like the story your mother told me in the park," John interjected.

"About the 'Widow's Coins'?" chimed in Marie, who had been quiet all this time.

"I heard another story this morning at the bodega around the corner that reminded me of the 'Widow's Coins' story," Annette said. "It was about how poinsettias came to be associated with Christmas…"

Annette retold Josefina's parable and then commented, "I think the moral is common to all cultures and religions. This morning, at the bodega, I realized that *'when it comes to giving, it's the thought that counts'* is a cliché, and so we discount it, but the reason a concept becomes a cliché is because it's *true*."

"I shared my painting supplies with your mother," John said. "And she told me my personal act of kindness reminded her of all that's right in the world."

"Yes," Marie said. "You *did* help me in that way."

"Way to go, John!" Annette grinned. "That's dharma in action! Tell me, how did it feel to know you'd made a difference for somebody in need?"

John pondered it. "It felt good. No! It felt *great*! I felt like I'd escaped from my own problems for a while. I guess the best word for it would be the phrase you've been using: I felt *connected*..."

He snapped his fingers. "It's like what they say: It really *is* better to give than to receive! I suppose that's another saying that became a cliché because it is so powerfully true, *if* we take the time to understand the meaning behind the words."

"Spoken like a Bodhisattva," Annette laughed.

"What does that term actually *mean*?" John asked.

"It means, 'being of wisdom,'" Marie interjected.

"I'm not *that*," John protested, blushing.

"We're *all* Bodhisattvas," Annette said. "The trick is to realize it."

The sound of breaking glass coming from the front yard disrupted the moment.

"My truck!" John exclaimed.

# 8. TURF WAR

John hurried outside with Annette right behind him to see his fears realized; the driver's side window of his truck had been shattered. A half-circle of youths stood gazing at the damage.

"What's going on?" John demanded.

A Black kid stepped forward wearing baggy denims and an over-sized blue hooded sweatshirt. He couldn't have been more than sixteen, but he matched John's height, and he held an aluminum baseball bat.

"Sorry about your truck," the teenager said. "I was *aiming* for his head!" He gestured with the bat at a scowling Asian kid dressed in warm up pants and jacket, who responded with a string of obscenities.

"I'm so sorry," Annette said to John. "Omar, how could you?"

"He crossed over into our turf," Omar said, dropping the bat.

"We've been over this a thousand times," Annette said. "This center belongs to everyone –"

"That's what you guys do?" John interrupted. "You hang around here daring each other to cross some imaginary line?"

"Yeah, so?" spoke up one of the Latino teens, who was wearing cargo pants and a sleeveless sweatshirt.

"What's your name?" John asked the Hispanic kid.

"Aarón."

"And you?" John looked at the Asian kid in the warm-up suit who'd been Omar's target.

"Ricky."

John glanced across the street. The clock in the window of a hardware store, the only open business in a row of abandoned storefronts, told him it was almost four. The afternoon was all but gone. So much of the day had been wasted in terms of his finding his true purpose as dictated by his vivid dream. Maybe he never would get to paint his masterpiece and realize his dream to be a great artist, but even if failure was his destiny, he might still be able to help Annette succeed with these kids…

The question was *how*?

Painting was all he knew… He'd used canvas and paints to help Annette's mother, but how could his artist's skills help in *this* situation?

He looked around the yard in frustration. His eyes fell upon the long, high, cinder block wall running the length of the youth center's front lot – and the idea came to him.

"Omar, you say you're better than Ricky and Aarón?" John asked.

"Me and my posse know we are," Omar replied defiantly.

"Then prove it," John said. He raised his voice. "All of you prove it!"

"How?" Omar demanded.

"By showing your colors," John said. "There!" He pointed at the wall. "Any of you guys tag?"

"We all do," Omar said, as the others nodded their heads in agreement.

"Whoa," Annette interjected. "I can't condone gang graffiti."

"I'm not talking about gang graffiti," John said. "I'm talking about these guys creating *burners*."

"What's that?" Annette asked.

"Dude's talking about real pictures," Omar said, smiling. "Stuff that burns off the wall and makes you notice it."

"That's right," John nodded. "We'll divvy up the wall into equal thirds. Each of you gets the same amount of space to bomb a mural to represent your culture –"

"*Bomb*?" Annette looked aghast.

"It means 'paint'," Ricky chuckled.

"You guys can create anything that can tell the world who you are and what you want out of life."

"I don't know…" Omar frowned.

"John?" Annette tugged at his sleeve.

"*We're* up for it," Ricky said, gesturing to his crew.

"Aarón?" John asked.

"Yeah, sure," Aarón replied. "We ain't afraid."

"John…" Annette repeated insistently.

"I guess that just leaves your posse, Omar," John challenged. "You in or out?"

"In!" Omar said, glaring at Ricky and Aarón.

"John!" Annette demanded.

"What?"

"What are we going to do for paint and stuff?"

"Huh?"

"I've been trying to tell you," Annette sighed. "I don't have supplies like that." She looked wistful. "Oh John, it was a great idea, it really was, but I don't have the money to buy all the supplies these kids would need to paint their murals."

"I knew it," Omar muttered. "Man *talks* big…"

*Annette looks absolutely heartbroken,* John thought, *beautiful but heartbroken.*

John thought Omar and the other kids looked equally disappointed. His idea to have them healthily compete by painting murals might just have actually worked…

"Look, you've been across the street from that hardware store forever," he told Annette. "Let's try to convince them to give us the stuff on credit."

"I guess it can't hurt to try," Annette said.

As they were crossing the street she asked, "This was your big idea. Don't you have a credit card?"

"Me? I'm a starving artist," John said. "I *had* one, but they took it away."

"Remind me not to go out to dinner with you," Annette said. "Not that you've asked me."

John swallowed hard. "Do you have a boyfriend?"

"I do *now*, huh?" Annette took his hand.

"I'm so comfortable with you," John said, marveling at his audacity. Usually he was shy with women. "How are you so *perfect*?"

"*We're* perfect. *Together*," Annette said. "It's scary weird, huh? In a *nice* way," she hurriedly added.

John's thoughts turned to his quickly dwindling day to find his purpose in life. "Do you believe in dreams?"

"Of course," Annette said as they entered the hardware store. "If you work hard enough, a dream can come true."

"I mean, do you believe that something in a dream that gets predicted, could actually happen?"

"You mean, like seeing the future?" Annette shrugged. "I don't know. I *guess* it's happened to somebody somewhere. Why do you ask?"

"It's a long story. I'll tell you later," John evaded. At least, he *hoped* he'd have the chance to tell her later.

The hardware store was a fluorescent-lit warren of metal shelving taken up with displays of hand tools, plumbing and electrical parts, and stacked bins of screws and bolts. John was relieved to see an entire wall of paints and brushes, with plenty of cans of spray paint.

The male proprietor behind the counter looked up from his newspaper propped against the cash register as John and Annette approached. He was swarthy, with several days' growth of beard, and wore a collarless tunic and pleated brimless cap.

"Yes, can I help you?" he asked them.

"We need paint. A lot of it," John said. "And brushes, and –"

"And some ladders" Annette chimed in, glancing at John. "The kids will need them, right?"

"It's for the youth center across the street," John said. "But we're a little short on cash, right now. Can we pay you later?" *Not that I have a clue how we'd ever actually be able to do that*, John thought to himself.

"I'm sorry. No paying later," the hardware proprietor said. "Come back when you have money," he said, returning to his newspaper.

John and Annette left the store, dejected.

# 9. GOOSENECK LAMP

"It was a great idea, John, it really was," Annette said as they stood on the sidewalk outside the hardware store. "I'll break the news to the kids."

"Wait," John said. "I want to go back in, alone. I want to try one more time to convince him to give us the paint and stuff we need."

"That's a lot for him to give us on credit." Annette looked doubtful.

"Not *loan* us, I mean *give* us," John said firmly. "I could never beg for anything for myself," John said. "But this is for others, and it's important. I have to try…"

Annette gazed at him, smiling. She suddenly threw her arms around his neck and kissed him lightly.

John's heart beat faster as he held her. "What was that for?"

"For good luck."

"I guess I should let go of you," he said.

"For now," Annette whispered. "So I can also give you *this* for good luck." She took something from the back pocket of her jeans.

He stared. It looked like the five dollar bill she'd told him about. The one Kanbun had given Hector on the island.

"Is that *Kanbun's* five bucks?" he asked.

Annette nodded. "It's always brought me luck," she murmured. "Maybe it will work for you, now."

John took the bill, not wanting to hurt her feelings, but he couldn't help wondering as he went back into the hardware store how the hell a measly five bucks could get them out of *this* jam…

"Yes? What is it, now?" the proprietor demanded.

"My name is John," he began, stalling, hoping for a bolt of inspiration to give him the words to convince this stranger to provide the paint supplies that were essential to his scheme to bring together the warring factions at the youth center. "May I ask your name?"

"It is Eshan," the proprietor said warily.

"Eshan, I want to explain to you why it is so important we get the painting supplies…"

John froze. Where were the words to get this guy to fork over the stuff? So much was riding on this. John couldn't bear to think he was going to screw this up too, the way he'd screwed up so much in his life…

He squeezed tight the folded up five-dollar bill Annette had given him, the five bucks that had been touched by Kanbun and Hector, and then Hector's wife, and then his granddaughter, Annette – and now lay in John's sweaty palm.

*Please let its magic work for me, too*, John fervently wished, or maybe even prayed. *Please, let it help me bridge this gap here and now*!

"You see the youth center across the street?" John began.

With the five-dollar bill squeezed in his fist, its good karma hopefully bolstering him, John explained his plan to have the gangs bridge their intolerance by painting murals. He heard himself explaining about the Charitable Lifeline to the silent shopkeeper, and how he had been taught this day to understand that mindful acts of charity are a powerful spiritual practice that could result in profound personal spiritual transformation.

The words seemed to pour out of John the way the paint would flow from his artist's brush when he was in the grip of fervent inspiration. When he was done, his mouth was parched. He felt mentally depleted and physically exhausted – the way he'd always imagined he would feel when he'd finally created his masterpiece.

"Here," John smoothed the five dollar bill out on the counter. "I know it doesn't seem like much, but it is very important to the woman who runs the center. I believe this scrap of paper has come to be imbued with great power. If you are at all a spiritual man, you may understand when I say I have come to think of it as something really quite precious, and I'm offering it you in exchange for the supplies we need to bring about change for the better in the lives of the teenagers across the street."

Eshan stared at the five dollar bill. "I will provide you with the supplies you need," he said softly.

"Really?"

"And please you should keep your talisman," Eshan added.

"I don't know how to thank you!"

Eshan held up his hand. "All I ask is that somewhere on the wall, you will make sure there is painted a black, gooseneck desk lamp."

John smiled brightly, wondering what the hell the guy was talking about. "A lamp… Sure… Anything with it? A desk blotter? Wastebasket?"

Eshan chuckled. "Now you will please allow *me* to explain. As you spoke to me just now I heard in your voice a passion that reminded me of a dearly departed friend."

"You mean somebody you know has died?" John asked. "I'm sorry, I didn't mean to joke…"

Eshan waved aside John's apology. "You see, next door, in the now vacant storefront, was a fix-it shop run by an old Jewish man. He died a year ago. Today, in fact, it is the anniversary of the tinker's death."

"What's a tinker?" John asked.

"Yes, I, too, had never before heard the term," Eshan acknowledged. "But that's what the old Jew called himself. He explained to me that a tinker is one who mended things. And he worked tirelessly at his trade. People brought their broken items to his fix-it shop from near and far. I myself am in my store from early morning to late at night, but no matter how early I arrived here, I would find the old man already bent over his work bench, muttering into his long, white beard as he worked. When I closed up in the evening, I would see him still working by the yellow pool of light cast from his black gooseneck desk lamp."

"He must have needed money," John remarked.

"No, it was not money he desired," Eshan said. "As I came to know him I found that he lived modestly and yearned for nothing… at least nothing material…"

"What do you mean?"

"Like you, I was puzzled as to what drove him. So I asked, 'Old man, why do you work so late at night, to fix cheap toasters and irons'?"

"What did he say?"

"Something, as it turns out, quite profound," Eshan replied. "Not that I realized it at the time. He told me, *'What I see, I can repair, and so bring about one less broken thing in the world.'*"

"I still don't understand," John said.

"Neither did I, at first." Eshan said. "However, the old man and I began to take tea together in the afternoons. At first, conversation was awkward. He was a Jew and I am a Muslim, after all. I won't bore you with our obvious differences of political opinion. What is much more interesting – to me, at least, and why I bring this story up – is where we found great areas of *agreement*, especially as concerns *acts of charity*."

"But what's the significance of the lamp?" John asked.

"It will hopefully come clear," Eshan said. "The old man told me of the Jewish tradition of *tzedakah*. He told me that *tzedakah* means righteousness, and that for Jews, charity is not an act of *generosity*, but of *justice* and *duty*. I told him about the similar Islamic traditions of *zakat* and *sadaqua*. The first is every good Muslim's obligation. It is tithing, giving a percentage of one's earnings. The second, *sadaqua*, is voluntary, in the sense that God gives us the choice to give more as a test of our characters. We are taught that this form of charity will be paid back to us in ways we may not immediately comprehend. *Sadaqua*, when practiced attentively, enriches the giver's life as much as the recipient's. We have a saying in this regard, '*A man giving a little during his life is better then a man who gives a lot at the moment of his death.*'"

It's the same moral as in the story about the little girl's humble but heartfelt gift of a bouquet of weeds that transformed into the poinsettia, John thought. And the story of the 'Widow's Coins.'

"I still don't get the lamp," John said.

"My friend the tinker told of the charitable tenet which most resonated inside his heart and by which he lived," Eshan said. "He called it *tikkun olam* – the duty to repair the world. The tinker said to me, *'When I came to America as a young man, this country was like a loving mother to me. Now, while I do not have wealth to give, I have my tinker's skills to use to repair the world. The poor families in this neighborhood can't afford to buy new appliances. So for them I fix for pennies – and sometimes for no charge – what would cost them precious dollars to replace. In this way a hard-working man before he leaves in the morning can have a piece of toast warm from the toaster I fixed. A mother can ease a difficult day listening to music on the radio I mended. And a child can study and learn without eye strain, thanks to the light from the lamp I repaired...'"*

Eshan paused. "I have come to think of the old tinker and *his* lamp that he used to light his workbench as a metaphor for how we should live. *'What I can see, I can repair,'* my friend said to me, *'So there is one less broken thing in the world....'"*

John nodded. "The metaphor of the tinker's lamp teaches us not to turn away from what we see broken."

"And just as important," Eshan added, "It reminds us that even if we help to bring about merely *one* less broken thing, that is a significant achievement. All the more so, because each time we repair something in the *world*, that mending is reflected in our own *spirit*."

"So when we deeply experience our own acts of repairing the world, we're also repairing ourselves," John offered.

"Quite so," Eshan agreed. "And so, to commemorate this first anniversary of my friend's death, I say to you, take what supplies you need from my shelves."

"Thank you," John said.

Eshan held up his hand. "Thank me by painting on your wall a resemblance of that old black gooseneck lamp the tinker sat by, so it shines brightly on the brave new world the teenagers depict."

"I will. I promise. You'll come over to see it."

"I look forward to it," Eshan smiled.

John paused. "You miss him a lot, don't you, your friend, the tinker, from next door?"

"You know," Eshan said softly, "The memory of walking past his shop in the twilight… seeing that old man by his lamp's soft glow fixing bit by bit what was broken in the world so as to restore a measure of joy to others… It was, I believe, the closest I have ever been to God's light."

# 10. BOMBS AWAY

The sun was low in the sky, casting long shadows across the youth center's asphalt lot as John mentored the teenagers on their project. The kids had created makeshift scaffolds out of some planks they'd found stacked up in the basement, and were busily laying out their concepts for their murals.

As it grew darker, and Annette turned on the building's outside security lights to illuminate the yard, Omar, Ricky and Aarón began to bicker over the fact that their respective factions felt they needed the lion's share of the wall to fully express their themes.

"Black people came to this city as slaves. We need to show that!" Omar argued.

"Asians worked the riverfront and we want to show it!" Ricky demanded.

"The factories couldn't have existed without my people!" Aarón insisted.

"Listen to each other!" John told them. "Your people each had a major role to play in making our city what it is today. Instead of each painting a small mural, why don't you all cooperate to create a single sweeping mural the entire length of the wall? Why not work *together* to show how the city wouldn't be here today if it weren't for what the Black, Latino and Asian citizenry contributed to our history!"

The trio of gang leaders looked at each other dubiously.

"I guess we could…" Omar said. He turned to John. "If you helped us lay it out?"

"You bet I will," John said. "I just need a space on the wall high up to paint something to fulfill a promise to a friend..."

Around seven o'clock, John was high on the scaffolding, tracing in the lamp he'd promised Eshan he would add to the mural, when he saw a panel truck nosing into the yard. His angle was such that he couldn't read what was written on the truck's side, but Annette, down below, didn't seem surprised to see its arrival.

"Who are those guys?" John yelled down to Annette, as two men exited the truck.

"A couple of repair men I called," Annette said. "I'll take care of it."

"Repair men," John repeated to himself and grinned, thinking again about what Eshan had told him about the old tinker who used to inhabit the shop next to the hardware store.

'...*That the old tinker and his lamp are a metaphor for how we should live... What I can see I can repair, so that there is one less broken thing in the world....*'

John was beginning to get a glimmer of how it was that broken people could also be repaired, just like refrigerators and TVs... That helping to fix *other folks* was how you could repair *yourself*....

In addition to the various fables he'd heard today, John thought about the story Annette had shared with him of her grandfather, Hector, turning his time on the island with Kanbun into a spiritual pilgrimage.

Hector had needed emotional repairs to find peace after his shoulder injury had stolen his baseball career...

And so *Kanbun* had helped to fix Hector's broken heart by giving of himself to the embittered ex-pitcher turned fighter pilot...

In turn, *Hector* had soothed the acute spiritual ache within *Kan-bun*, a gentle scholar involuntarily sent to war, who longed to step out from the giant shadow cast by his illustrious great, great, great grandfather Kōbō Daishi…

*Everything I've experienced and heard about today has to do with giving*, John thought. *And how when you focus on giving, you get something incredibly valuable in return.*

Over the years, he'd done some exploring of spirituality. He'd tried to get back into the Catholicism he'd grown up with, dabbled in Zen, and read self-help books in his desperation to find some inner peace and tranquility – all to mesh the reality of what he *was* in the world with the lofty ideal he felt driven to *be*.

Zen masters put forth that enlightenment came through remembering what we already know. John surmised that his experiences this past day were teaching him a very elementary but eternal truth about *giving* that each of us already knew: *whether you give five bucks or five million – or just a few hours of your time – you are simply doing a favor.*

As soon as this idea popped into his head, it excited him. He knew that people certainly felt good about themselves when they did a favor for family or friends…

*Why couldn't everyone feel the same pleasurable rush when they were giving to charity that they feel when they fulfilled a personal favor to a loved one or friend?*

And then John pondered the old tinker's words as relayed to him by Eshan…

'*What I can see I can repair, so there is one less broken thing in the world….*'

"And since the world is merely a reflection of our inner state of being," John said out loud to himself. "When we repair the world – or save the world – we're really repairing – saving – *ourselves*."

All it took was a shift in one's perspective to continually experience this same contentment, serenity and bliss from giving that John was currently experiencing through his work this night, on the wall.

If more people could attain this perspective shift, might their pleasure further motivate them to find additional ways to give – to connect – and maybe tip the collective balance of positive energy in the world?

*We could as individuals and as the family of man prosper in mind, body and spirit,* John realized, *by devoting ourselves to saving the world on say, no more than five bucks worth of charity – be it money or time – a day."*

"Save the world on five dollars a day," John savored the words. "I like the sound of that…"

"Yo! John!" Omar yelled from the opposite end of the wall. "We could use you over here to plan out this section of the mural."

"Glad to help," John said.

*Glad. To. Help.*

# 11. SUNDAY GRAVY BRAINSTORM

"They're just couple of repair men I called," Annette reluctantly fibbed to John as the Bender Realty truck with the two men she'd shooed away that morning, returned as promised.

"I can take care of it," Annette had added, wondering how in the world she was going to make good on *that* fib…

They were back for their pasta dinner, Annette knew, and to take inventory of the salvageable materials from the soon to be demolished youth center.

She felt guilty about keeping the bleak fate of the youth center from John, but he'd seemed so turned on by what he was accomplishing with the kids that she just didn't have the heart to tell him – or the teenagers working so hard on their mural – that their work wasn't destined to last.

Besides, even if the mural was going to be demolished, maybe the camaraderie it was inspiring among the different groups would endure.

She thought back to *Nonno* Hector on the island with Kanbun, who came to understand the value of the calligraphy the two men painstakingly rendered each day, only to have the tropical rains wash their work away…

Annette hoped deep in her heart that somehow, as with that fated-to-be ephemeral calligraphy on the island, the benefit of all this was going to come from the *doing of it*.

In the kitchen, she put water on to boil for the pasta and turned up the heat on the long simmering pot of *Nonna* Rita's Sunday gravy. Meanwhile, the two Bender workmen poked around the building, making notes on their clipboards. When supper was ready she called the guys into the kitchen and seated them around the old, chrome and red vinyl kitchenette set.

"Lady, this is the best," said the curly-haired, broad shouldered guy between mouthfuls. He looked like he could really pack away the food.

"Is there more?" the littler, bald guy with glasses piped up, proffering a hopeful look along with his empty bowl.

"I'm ready for more, too," Curly said.

"Did you find a lot of stuff that was valuable?" Annette asked as she ladled gravy on second helpings for both.

"Copper pipes," Baldy replied, wiping stray specks of *Nonna*'s gravy from his glasses. "That stuff's worth plenty on the salvage market."

"That's how Bender made his first million," Curly interjected, digging into his pasta.

"Do you know when the building is slated to be demolished?" Annette asked.

"They don't tell us that stuff," Curly said.

"Do you know what Bender is going to build here?"

Curly shrugged. "Like I said, that stuff's beyond our pay grade."

"I never even met Bender," Baldy said "Seen him around, though."

"He's kind of a Scrooge," Curly agreed. "He stomps around with a sourpuss – you really don't want to attract his attention"

"Amen to *that*," Baldy nodded vigorously. "I don't suppose I could have thirds?" he asked meekly.

"He's got a hollow leg," Curly laughed.

"Would you like thirds as well," Annette smiled.

"No thanks. It was really delicious," he said, and then his grin faded. "You know, we are sorry about what we've been ordered to do. It seems like you got a nice place going here. Those kids working on that wall painting, and all…"

"Yeah, it's a shame," Baldy agreed, peering at Annette over his coke-bottle specs. "But it's Bender's world, we just get to live in it."

"You know," Curly began. "One thing I *do* know about Bender is that he cares about his public image. I think if you called the local TV station and got them to do a story on that community wall painting project you got going on…"

"You're a genius!" Annette exclaimed. "In the past, I've tried to get the media involved in my cause, but they've always turned me down saying it just wasn't exciting enough. But the mural project might be just the ticket to capture public attention and get popular opinion on my side."

"I wish you luck," Curly said as he and Baldy gathered up their clipboards and flashlights in preparation for leaving. "Just don't say you got the idea from us!"

# 12. BODHISATTVAS WITH PAINT BRUSHES

It was nine o'clock that evening, and John was still working on the wall. He was sharing the scaffolding with a slender, intent-looking Latina named Estela, who was wearing jeans and a tee shirt advertising a local karate school.

"So you study karate?" John asked, feeling the need to make conversation.

"I do," Estela said. "A lot of the women in the neighborhood take it to show the boys we are their equal and more," she said proudly. "I'm going for my black belt, next month." She studied John. "You look familiar. Have I seen you in the bodega?"

"The one around the corner?"

"Yeah," Estela said. "It belongs to my grandparents. I live with them above the store and I work there on the weekends, cleaning the place and helping my grandfather take the perishable food we didn't sell to the local food bank."

"You give all that stuff away?"

Estela shrugged. "Better than throwing it away, right? Sure, it's a lot of work loading the stuff into the truck and driving it to the food bank instead of just tossing it in the dumpster, but it feels good after it's been done, you know? It's like working out at the dojo – hard while you're doing it, but it feels good after."

"You into the spiritual aspect of the martial arts?"

"Oh, yeah, you *got* to be," Estela said. "My *Sensei* says that Karate's like a three-leg stool. The legs are mind, body and spirit –" She grew steadily more enthusiastic as she warmed to the subject. "If you're missing one of the stool's legs, your karate is going to be weak and wobbly. Plus, your martial arts practice doesn't end when you leave the dojo! I figure I'm strengthening my mind, body and spirit when I'm loading up our truck with leftover groceries to take to the food bank."

John nodded. "I've been thinking that what we're doing here is all about mind, body and spirit, as well. You know, there are different paths to enlightenment, which is a transformation of your inner self. For some it's meditation… for others it's martial arts… and for artists, it can be the act of creation…"

"I follow you," Estela said.

"I've been thinking that the act of giving – if done in a mindful way – could be another path. Right now we're giving with our minds, our bodies and our spirits to create this mural. It's work on a physical level – like doing karate or loading your truck with stuff to take to the food bank – that also pays off on a spiritual level."

"Right!" Estela said. "But you got to pay attention to what you're doing and not just go through the motions. My *Sensei* also says if we just go through the motions during our workouts, it's a waste of time and energy. We got to practice mindfulness as well as kicks and punches to really learn it."

"Mindfulness," John nodded. "That's the key, all right…"

*If we strive to develop mindfulness in our charitable giving,* he thought, *if we allow ourselves to fully experience each aspect and nuance of the ritual of giving, from contemplating the request… deciding to give... and then making a contribution of time or money – all the steps that comprised Annette's Charitable Lifeline – our act of goodness will far more powerfully resonate within us.*

"You know," Estela continued. "Being up here, working on this mural, it really *is* like being in karate class. I love working out because it gets me out of myself. While I'm being mindful of what I'm doing at the dojo, I'm not thinking about my own problems."

"I hear you," John said.

"And when I *do* find myself thinking about my problems," Estela added. "They somehow don't seem so *bad*. Another thing that gets me out of stressing on my problems is to help others. Like the other day? When I was demonstrating a technique to a junior student? *Sensei* commented that I was strengthening my own karate."

Estela paused. "Sensei said, '*The spirit will always remember the acts of the heart.*'"

As John pondered the girl's words, he was distracted as a news van from the local television station pulled into the yard, parking in the space vacated by the repair truck that had come and gone hours ago. The news crew quickly set up floodlights as the chatting, laughing teens, wielding brushes and cans of spray paint, continued to swarm over the wall.

John wiped wet paint from his hands with a turpentine soaked rag and climbed down from the scaffolding. He walked over to Annette, as the correspondent in her bright blue blazer smiled into the camera and began her broadcast.

"Who called them?" he asked.

"I did," Annette said. "I want the city to know the wonderful thing you're doing here."

"Me?" John asked, startled.

"Uh-huh, and guess what?" Annette said. "The TV news lady wants to interview you."

"I'm busy helping the kids," he protested. "*You* talk to them."

"*You're* the man of the hour," Annette told him. "Here she comes!"

"Stay with me, at least," he implored Annette.

"Always," she said, taking his hand as the news correspondent approached with her camera crew in tow.

"Always, *really*?" John asked, his heart pounding.

Annette nodded, looking into his eyes. John desperately wanted to kiss her.

But then the correspondent was peppering him with questions –

*"How did you get the idea to bring these kids together?*

*"What do you hope to accomplish?*

*"Do you really believe this can make a difference?"*

The floodlights made John squint as the microphone was thrust into his face. It was scary to be the center of so much attention.

"Annette… I don't know what to say," he muttered.

"Just tell them what's in your heart."

She squeezed his hand – rather like the way he'd squeezed that five-dollar bill she'd given him for luck in persuading Eshan, at the hardware store – and once again John felt a surge of indomitable confidence and conviction pouring into him.

"Well, to answer your last question first, I *do* think this can make a difference," he began. "This past day, I've met some incredible people and each one of them, in their way, has impressed me with the fact that every one of us can make a significant difference and better the world. And those people I met have taught me something else," he continued. "I always knew that all of us were *supposed* to be charitable to help others… to do our *best* to be *decent* in an *impossible* world… But today, I've come to realize that giving to others is a *great way to help yourself!*" As John spoke he felt Annette gently disengage her hand from his.

"You go, Bodhisattva," she murmured, stepping away.

"What about people who don't have much to give?" the TV correspondent asked.

"It's not about *amount*," John said. "It's about *intent*…

"*Caring* not *currency*…

"*Mindfulness* not *money*…

"Once you realize this," John elaborated. "Then your contributions, no matter how modest, can make an incredible difference in how you view yourself − your sense of self worth − and your relation to the world. I've been thinking about it in terms of five dollars. That's not really very much in the scheme of things, right?"

"Not much at all," the correspondent agreed.

"So let's think of the 'five bucks' as a *symbol* for how little we need to give in order to receive the infinite peace and serenity that comes from a transformed perception of ourselves and the world. "Again, the key is not how *much* we give, but to experience our giving as *meditation*."

"It sounds awfully mystical," the correspondent said.

"Not at all," John said. "After all, meditation is just a way to reprogram your brain to think a different way. When Norman Vincent Peale wrote *The Power of Positive Thinking,* back in the fifties, all he was advocating was to change your thinking by reprogramming your brain through the practice of positive imagery, right?"

"I suppose you're right," the correspondent replied.

"And since then, a lot's been written about the power of positive imagery to realize your dreams," John continued. "So all I'm saying is, to *deeply contemplate* the significance of your decision to make a charitable gift of time or money, is *another* way of leveraging the power of positive thinking to change your mindset and feel better about yourself. And maybe another way to think about *karma,* is to consider it merely another name for the law of attraction: through our charitable acts we're practicing good karma, and so good things will be attracted to us."

John smiled at the correspondent. "Just imagine if we *all* did that! We could heighten our collective consciousness and bring about a transformation in the world."

"You sound like you're speaking from personal experience," observed the correspondent.

"I am," John replied. "Yesterday I felt like a failure. My life was unsatisfying, my dreams had turned to ashes and my connection to the world was non-existent. I was lonely and miserable. I think all of us at some point in our lives have suffered at least one traumatic setback. It might be a professional failing… a relationship come apart… or some other disappointment that freezes us in negativity, like a fossilized creature trapped in a block of amber. But I've discovered that the more I think about my acts of charity, the more it helps me to feel better about my self-worth and connectivity to the world. I feel my inner darkness dissolving in the light and warmth generated by my giving. That light and warmth melts the amber and sets me free!"

"*Now* you're sounding very *religious,*" the correspondent commented, her observation momentarily stymying John.

"You know, I hadn't really thought about that aspect of it," he said. "It's true that a lot of what's been imparted to me today has to do with relating to God, but I don't think that practicing mindful giving as a way to feel better about yourself and become one with the world *requires* you to be religious. You can approach it purely in a secular, pragmatic way – like deciding to eat a healthier diet or instituting a program of physical exercise. When I go out for a run, for instance, I end up feeling pretty good. A scientist would say it's because the physical exertion caused a release of endorphins in my body. In the same sort of way, I think mindful giving releases something like endorphins. It brings about a pleasurable change in your way of thinking by reprogramming your mind to more positively view the world and your place within it."

The news correspondent had been nodding animatedly throughout John's explanation. "However, if you *are* religious," she offered, "I imagine mindful giving is a way to strengthen and solidify your relationship with the Almighty..."

"That's right," John said and paused. "I've devoted my life to painting. I always wanted to change the world with my art, and now I think that maybe I *can*... by sharing my art through acts of giving like what's taking place here, today. As a result, I will reap the benefit of feeling better about myself. That's *my* five buck contribution to saving the world, and I think it's a small price to pay for so much in return."

The phrase that had popped into John's head earlier that evening came back to him. "That's what I'm doing here... I'm trying to *change* my view of myself and the world: to *save the world, on five dollars a day."*

"Thank you, John," the correspondent smiled. She turned to the camera. "We've been speaking with a true artist who's been teaching us 'How to Save the World on Five Dollars a Day.'"

# 13. JOHN'S MASTERPIECE

John worked with the teenagers throughout the rest of the night to complete the mural. At some point, just before dawn, he went back to his truck intending to rest his eyes for just a few minutes.

The next thing he knew it was daylight. He'd had the strangest dream, the second in as many nights… In it, he'd been about to embark on an eagerly anticipated trip with Annette, but he was late for the plane. He was going to miss the trip, but a crowd of people he didn't know came together to get him to the airport by hiring a black Mercedes limo to speed him on his way. The limo driver was dressed smartly in a blue suit and maroon tie, but John never caught a glimpse of his face…

And then he'd woken up.

John got out of his truck, stretching and yawning, and went over to where Annette was watching as the kids put their finishing touches on the mural.

"You didn't sleep?" he asked, putting his arm around her shoulder.

"No, I was too excited by all this," she said, leaning against him "I've worked here for years trying to achieve what you did in one night. So what do you think of your masterpiece?"

"My what?" John stared at her.

"Your masterpiece," Annette repeated. "Why are you looking at me like that?"

"It's just that… Well, I had a dream where I was told I had to figure some things out… and I presumed that it meant I had to paint my masterpiece…"

"Well," Annette said softly, kissing him on the cheek. "I think your dream came true. Just look at what you've accomplished!"

It was true, John realized. In a way, he *had* brought about the creation of an artistic masterpiece…

The expanse of wall had been transformed overnight into a grand and all encompassing mural chronicling the city and its people's history. The teenagers had depicted Black slaves, Asian factory workers and Latino dockhands as literally the pillars of the community. The arms of these disparate groups reached up, spreading and morphing into the branches of a single, ancient and mighty tree that supported the city as it was today. Men and women from the various ethnic groups – doctors, business people, soldiers and police officers – populated this depiction of the city, while children played together upon a multi-colored rainbow that spanned like a bridge behind and between the city's skyline.

And over it all, shining rays of golden light, was a black, gooseneck desk lamp of a sun.

"It's wonderful, all right," John said, his voice choked with emotion. He pulled Annette close. "But there's the *real* masterpiece."

He pointed to where the teenagers gazing at their mural were no longer standing in segregated gangs, but intermingled. They were laughing and joking with one another as friends, at long last.

John glanced across the street to see that the hardware store was already open for business. Eshan hadn't been kidding when he said he worked long hours. "I'll be right back," he said. "I want to get Eshan so he can see what he helped to bring about."

John sprinted across the lot and stepped off the curb, his thoughts taken up with how pleased he hoped Eshan would be to see the old Jewish tinker's lamp lighting up the world of the mural. He was half-way across the street when he looked to his left and paused, trans-fixed by the sight of a gleaming black Mercedes limo parked on the opposite curb.

"Just like my dream," John said to himself.

Any nice car in this poor neighborhood would be out of place, but a Mercedes limo was exceptionally incongruous. The driver in his black suit and cap was leaning against the fender when he suddenly began wildly gesticulating to John.

As John turned he noticed the clock in the hardware store's front window.

It was 8:02 AM

His one day, as prophesied in his dream, had passed.

"John, look out!" Annette screamed.

He caught a flash of yellow out of the corner of his eye as the cab hurtled toward him in a cacophony of roaring engine, blaring horn and screeching brakes. There was no time to react. John closed his eyes.

*Annette, I love you*, he thought.

His heart and soul was suffused with deep sadness and longing for all that he was going to miss, and yet he felt an incredible sense of contentment concerning the good he had done –

And then he was flying through the air and hurtling toward the curb.

# 14. RECONCILIATION

"John, look out!" Annette screamed.

She watched horrified, as John, standing in the middle of the street, didn't realize he was directly in the path of a speeding taxi.

She was certain he was going to be killed, but then a man in a blue suit bolted from the backseat of the Mercedes limo to grab John by the collar of his sweatshirt and jerk him out of the cab's path, far quicker and more forcefully than John could have moved on his own.

John sprawled back, the cab whizzing past and just missing his legs as he tumbled into the gutter, but the man in the blue suit was behind him, breaking John's fall, preventing John's skull from cracking against the curb.

Annette was at John's side in an instant, kneeling beside him. "Are you okay?" she asked frantically, cradling his head.

"Yes, I'm fine, thanks to –" John was turning his head to see who had saved him.

"Thank you so much," Annette began, gazing up at the man. "You?" she gasped. It was the old man she had rescued from drowning yesterday morning. Except that today he was clean-shaven and wearing an expensive blue suit and maroon patterned tie.

"Dad?" John blurted, staring up at the man.

"*Dad?*" Annette echoed.

She swiveled her gaze between the two men. "What is going on here?"

"I guess I got here in the nick of time," the old man said.

"Who *are* you?" Annette demanded.

"Yesterday I didn't tell you my name," he said. "I was ashamed to tell you, after you saved me from making such a tragic mistake. And I would have been *doubly ashamed* to tell you if I'd known at the time who *you* really were."

"Who I am is really *confused*," Annette complained.

"My name is William Bender, of Bender Realty Trust. I'm the man who's been doing his utmost to shut this youth center down and turn it into a parking lot for a stadium I intend to build."

He gestured to John. "And this is my son."

"*Disowned* son," John glowered, getting to his feet and brushing himself off.

"But yesterday you looked like a bum," Annette stammered. "And why were you trying to kill yourself?"

"Dad?" John went pale. "You were trying to do *what*?"

Bender looked away, clearly embarrassed. "Annette, yesterday, when you found me at the pier, I hadn't been home for days. I hadn't eaten or slept. I was so distraught over losing my son…"

"He means my older brother, Don, who was killed in Iraq," John said sourly.

"No," Bender countered. "I was able to make my peace with God over Donald's death a *long time ago*. Besides, I can never lose him because he will always be in my heart."

He put his hands on John's shoulders. "It was *you* I couldn't get over losing."

"Me?" John stammered.

"What *happened* between you two?" Annette demanded.

"I haven't seen my father since Don's funeral," John said. "When we had a terrible falling-out."

"It was my fault." Bender said. "I drove John away from me. He always wanted to be an artist and I initially encouraged him to fulfill his dream. You see, I had always counted on Donald coming into the business with me, but after he was killed in Iraq, I expected John to rise to the call and fill Don's shoes. He refused and I said terrible things to John."

Bender locked eyes with John. "They were things I never should have said and never truly believed, Son," he continued. "I guess I was haunted by Don's ghost…"

John, swallowing hard, took up the story. "After our blowout at the funeral, I cut all my ties with Dad. I was determined to make it as an artist and prove to him that I was *every bit the winner* that Don was, in my *own* way." He looked at his father. "But why *now*, Dad? Why the change of heart *now*?"

Bender looked down at his expensive polished shoes. "Last night I had a dream… it was wonderful and terrible at the same time, because Donald was in it, but what he had to say to me was so frightening."

"John?" Annette murmured. "Are you sure you're okay? That you didn't hit your head on the curb or something?'

"I'm okay," John said softly.

"But you're so white," Annette persisted. "Like you've seen a ghost…"

"What happened in *your* dream, Dad?" John asked.

## 15. HOW TO SAVE THE WORLD
## ON $5 A DAY

"I can still vividly see every detail of my dream," Bender said. "Donald came to me in my office. He was in his uniform. He stood beside my desk, where I keep the wooden box containing the folded flag that dressed his coffin. With his back to the wall where I have his medals displayed, he warned me that I only had this day to make up with John…"

Bender shook his head in wonderment. "I figured he was saying *I* only had a short while. I never guessed he meant it was *John* whose life was in danger!"

"How did you come to be *here now*, Mister Bender" Annette asked.

"First of all, none of that, Mister stuff," Bender insisted. "Call me Bill. I came here to see you and John. After my dream I couldn't go back to sleep, so I turned on the TV and saw the news report of what you were doing with these kids. Then I just had to come down to see you both –"

"This is just too freaky," John interrupted. "You see, Dad, I had a dream about Don, too…"

After John finished recounting his dream, he added, "So what do you think, Dad? Annette just said I looked like I'd seen a ghost. Maybe I *have*. Maybe we both *have*."

"Son, I think we both saw an *angel*."

"What matters," Annette interjected. "At least, what I *hope* matters, is that you both realize you need to make up with each other!"

"She's right," Bill said. "I love you, John. Whatever you want to do with your life is fine with me, as long as we can be father and son again."

"I want that too, Dad," John whispered, embracing his father.

"What an incredible day this last 24 hours has been," Annette marveled.

"The *most* incredible day," John exclaimed.

Bill nodded. "In my dream, Donald reminded me of the fragility of life, and that I had *only a day* to make amends –"

"*Only a day* to find my true purpose," John chimed in.

"*Only a day* to save this youth center from *your* wrecking ball, Bill," Annette said.

"If *everybody* realized we only have this day," Bill mused, "How might our values and the way we conduct ourselves be different?"

John felt a chill run down his spine as he recalled Don's telling him: *'I'm giving you the greatest gift anyone can give: Self awareness.'*

"And as to that wrecking ball," Bill continued. "You needn't worry about it any longer, young lady."

"Really?" Annette asked. "Bill, are you saying you're going to spare the youth center?"

"More than spare it," Bill replied. "From what I saw on the news, you've accomplished something momentous on behalf of these kids, so I've come here to make you a proposition."

"I don't understand, Dad," John said.

"That makes two of us," Annette said, taking John's hand.

"I want you to do what you did here all across the country," Bill continued. "I'm prepared to fund an organization where you'll help people from all walks of life use art to better their lives and the world."

"Dad, that's very kind of you, but I wouldn't know how to manage a program like that…" John began.

"*I* would," Annette said.

"There you go," Bill grinned. "Son, I did a little fact checking on our Annette… Did you know this young lady has undergraduate and graduate degrees from Harvard in urban planning and business administration? She is more than qualified in my estimation to administrate a program of the size I envision."

"How large a program are you talking about, Bill?" Annette asked.

"Oh, I'll fund it at five million, I figure," Bill said.

Annette gasped.

"Just as seed money," Bill said, sounding apologetic. "Until you get things up to speed, which shouldn't be long now that the public as caught on to 'How to Save the World on Five Dollars a Day,' as John named it when he was interviewed on TV last night."

"The public's caught on?" John repeated. "I don't understand…"

"Then you haven't seen the news?" Bill asked.

John shook his head. "Why? What's going on?"

"That story has been picked up by the media – it's all anybody is talking about," Bill said. "It seems everybody wants to know more about what you're saying… That all of us can learn how to practice mindfulness while performing acts of charity and reap the personal benefits. Your idea of being fully invested in the moment in order to give not just with one's *wallet,* but also with one's *heart and mind* is really resonating."

"Check it out, man," Omar said, approaching with Aarón. He held out his iPhone, where the video of John's previous night's TV interview was playing on the diminutive screen. "It's gone viral on You-Tube."

"I already spoke with some advertising people," Bill said. "They all agree that 'How to Save the World on Five Dollars a Day,' with its emphasis on positive change in the community, is going to be huge with Baby Boomers, who are into the idea of having it all; not just material wealth, but spiritual fulfillment, as well. These marketing guys say the Baby Boomers demand accountability, and like to see the results of their generosity. That's why Baby Boomers are more likely to give to a local food bank, to sponsor a community project, or to their house of worship." Bill added. "Those ad guys are experts, so they must know what they're talking about."

"It works like this, Dad," John said:

*"One – when you write a check or decide to volunteer, remember that the charitable organization itself is merely a conduit; that you're connecting with the people the charity is set up to help. In essence, you're simply doing someone a favor;*

*"And Two – Once you make that contribution, stop and savor the favor you bestowed – or blessing if you prefer the term. Pat yourself on the back by contemplating your generosity. Allow the good thing you did to reinforce your own positive self-image and change your perspective on yourself and the world."*

"That's how you save yourself," Annette said. "It's also how you save the world – *your* world – by seeing things in a whole new light."

"Hey, Annette!" Aarón exclaimed. "Ricky said to tell you he's setting up a Facebook page for 'How to Save the World on Five Dollars a Day.' And you guys also need to be on Twitter. You going to have a humongous following!"

Bill said, "With Annette administrating and John as spokesperson, we'll be flooded with donations and folks who want to volunteer to lend a hand. I never knew you had such a presence on camera, Son."

"It's his artist's passion," Annette said.

"But I'm a failed artist," John protested.

"Son, a successful artist creates," Bill said. "And you've created enduring harmony and beauty where there was none before."

"And an artist's work endures for generations," Annette added. "Your work in the community of the world will continue to grow and inspire."

"An artist creates beauty," Bill continued. "Your canvas is now the world."

"Are you all right?" Annette murmured as John's eyes grew wet.

"I'm fine," John said, embracing her. "I'm just so grateful on this day to have found *you*, and to have found my *purpose* in life, after all. It's to spread the word on *How to Save the World on Five Dollars a Day*."

# AFTERWORD

Annette and John discover that through acts of personal philanthropy, it is possible to heal and transform oneself and the world. The key, say the people they meet, who express it according to Christian, Buddhist, Judaic and Islamic points of view, is to be fully invested in the moment in order to give not just with one's wallet, but also with one's heart and mind.

If we strive to develop such heartfelt mindfulness, if we allow ourselves to fully experience each aspect and nuance of the ritual of giving, from contemplating the request... deciding to give... the act of writing the check, or in some other way transferring the contribution... then our act of goodness will far more powerfully resonate within us.

This was once a well-known benefit of living – and loving one another – according to the "Golden Rule." But the wisdom has since been lost to humankind as our living arrangement has greatly transformed from a rural, village based society where neighbor helping neighbor was the basis of the social contract, to the anonymous, urban/suburban transient lives that most of us lead today.

Can you imagine how satisfying it must have been for everyone who participated in an old-fashioned barn raising? To be on the receiving end of a neighbor's grateful appreciation, and to have the serene certitude that when *your* time of need came around, your community would be there for you?

Today, the barn-raising experience is the hallmark of several well-known humanitarian organizations, for example, Habitat for Humanity, where volunteers come together to build or restore housing for low-income families under the guidance of construction professionals.

(I've volunteered to work at Habitat for Humanity build sites, and I can testify first hand that the experience of directly helping to bring about life-changing circumstances for others is uniquely affecting.)

Clearly, however, not everyone has the time or inclination to volunteer to help build a house, serve meals in a shelter, deliver humanitarian aid in a Third World country, and so on.

Many of us when we want to give, prefer to be check writers rather than doers…

To that end, in these last few pages you'll find some additional tips on how to approach making your *financial* charitable contributions in a way that will be conducive to realizing and enjoying all the benefits of *your* personal philanthropy.

**See the Human Face of the Charity** – Remember that despite what you write on the "Pay To" line of your check, you are not giving to that organization, or to the charity's staff or volunteers, as wonderful as these people may be. You are not even giving to the charity's laudable cause. *You are giving to the people who the charity helps.*

This holds true even when you give to a health charity to support research to cure a terrible disease. View your donation not as supporting the research, but towards improving and saving lives by bringing about new treatments and cures that much sooner.

Put another way, your money doesn't ultimately help the researcher in her white lab coat peering into a microscope. It helps the man, woman or child in the doctor's office who are or will be receiving the treatment that your involvement helps make possible. You have helped make *that treatment possible as much as the efforts of any researcher.*

**Be In Control** – Here's a jolting revelation from a professional fundraiser: You don't have to give every time you're asked. Even more astounding, nobody, *including the charity,* expects you to!

It's human nature to feel a twinge when you throw away a charity's solicitation, and even more difficult to say no when they call you on the phone. But the truth is, your charity will understand and you can consider yourself a loyal donor and compassionate person if you give only a few times a year to any particular charity. (Although I do think it's easier to experience the joys of giving as outlined in this book by making frequent smaller contributions – whatever you can afford – as opposed to an infrequent larger donation.)

Think of each charitable request that you receive as if it were a bus traveling your desired route. There might be a bus going by your stop every fifteen minutes. Nobody expects you to take them all. The frequency of the buses allows you to ride more or less on your schedule. It's the same with charitable requests – give according to *your* schedule.

Again, the best way to experience the benefits of giving according to your financial situation is to make, say, five ten dollar gifts rather than one fifty dollar gift... or ten fifty dollar gifts instead of one five hundred dollar gift... This is just like the way you'll get more out of exercising an hour a day five days a week, as opposed to exercising five hours each weekend.

To reiterate: nobody expects you to give each and every time you're asked (although charities can certainly well-use the money, and would be ecstatic if you did!) Simply donate at your financial comfort level, parceling out the amounts of your contributions so you can frequently receive the mental and spiritual paybacks of charitable giving.

**Be Loyal** – It may sound odd to think of being loyal to a charity the way you might be loyal to your favorite sports team, but those who get the most out of giving are those who are their cause's greatest fans.

Find a charity that resonates with you and stick with it. Build connections between yourself and the cause by spending time on its website, exploring links, perhaps advocating on its behalf, participating in its events (walks, runs, biking, etc.), and maybe even eventually volunteering.

Or, simply contribute financially, but root for your charity to 'win' – and you'll experience far more emotional pleasure when your charity shares with you the good news of victories earned with your help, and personal involvement when you're informed of challenges still to be met.

**Form a Giving Club** – Giving Clubs are like Investment Clubs – except instead of communally investing in stocks and bonds for monetary profit, you're investing in a good cause for emotional and spiritual profit. It can be as small as your immediate family, or it can encompass the neighborhood. As with investment clubs, by pooling your money with others you can make an even bigger difference in your favorite cause. The ancillary benefit includes the opportunity to connect or reconnect with your spouse, children, parents, siblings, friends and neighbors on topics that go above and beyond your immediate day-to-day personal concerns.

Enjoy the rich exchange of ideas, aspirations and dreams for oneself and the world by forming or joining a giving club – and experience the community spirit that was once our social obligation and our recompense, back when community barn-raisings were the norm.

I'll leave you with…

## The 10 Benefits Offered to You in *How to Save the World on $5 a Day*

**1. Connecting to the World** – Our charitable acts of reaching out to one another make us all 'family,' and in the process, tear down the walls that we build around ourselves with the bricks and mortar of life's hard knocks and disappointments. Mystics struggle for years to feel at one with the universe. You can feel that way by fully savoring every phase of your charitable acts as you travel along Annette's Charitable Lifeline as discussed in the parable:

*"Generosity → Giving → Positive action → Gratitude → Satisfaction"*

**2. Making a Difference** – Everybody wants to make a difference. The best way for us to actually *make* that difference and help change the world – save the world – is through charitable giving.

Yes, the act of giving will change your own perspective, but it will obviously also pragmatically help *others* in need, and in that way brighten the future for us *all*. Your gifts of money or time in any amount will help better the world at large.

So practice your personal philanthropy and take your place alongside Bill Gates, Warren Buffet and other important philanthropists who are making a world-changing difference.


**3. Receiving Recognition** – Next to *"I love you,"* the most meaningful and profound words a person can hear are *"Thank you."* Receiving an expression of gratitude conveys that you've indeed connected and made a difference… that you've performed a rescue and are, at that moment, a hero.

The acclaimed tennis player and social activist Arthur Ashe said, *"True heroism is remarkably sober, very undramatic. It is not the urge to surpass all others at whatever cost, but the urge to serve others at whatever cost."*

Do you want to feel like a hero? Do you want to *be* a hero? Myriad opportunities await you every day of your life to be heroic through personal philanthropy.


**4. Fulfilling Moral and Religious Aspirations** – This point goes almost without saying. The parable provides an overview of the history and traditions of altruism across different cultures and religions. The fact is, if you are a religious person, the most meaningful way to transform your outlook and your own circumstances, is to put your religious belief into practice and feel God with you, by mindfully doing God's work to reach out to those less fortunate.

**5. Strengthening the Social Fabric** – The social fabric of the world is undeniably torn and frayed, but each of us can help mend it by acts of giving. If you heard a call for help in the next room, would you ignore it? Of course you wouldn't. But what if the cry for help came from across the street, or from the other side of town? What if that frightened, hurting person who needed you was *on the other side of the world?*

A charitable organization I worked with sent food and medicine to help the people of Pakistan after the 2008 earthquake. Many of the quake's victims were deeply grateful to Americans for their generosity. They came to view Americans as friends, with positive international implications for years to come. That's the kind of strengthening of the social fabric that is so important to our planet's future.

Bottom line: When we give of our time and money to those in need, we strengthen those whom we help, we strengthen ourselves and we strengthen the social fabric of the community (which might be your neighborhood, the town, or the slightly larger community in which we live that goes by the name of Planet Earth.)

**6. Investing in the Future** – Would you like to leave a lasting legacy to the world? Your gifts of time and money to good causes will truly make a difference today and for future generations. Many people accomplish this through "planned giving," which is a substantial and significant donation to a charitable organization that is integrated into the giver's personal, financial and estate planning goals, and which ensures that the individual's charitable impulses will endure after they are gone.

However, the littlest change for the better in the world – right now – is equally important as a sizeable planned gift designed to benefit posterity. When you make even the smallest contribution you are improving things, and your contribution, when joined with others, creates a chain reaction that is all powerful and without end to change the future for the better.

The lesson of this book is that *intent is everything*. It is our *intent* to give and *awareness* of our acts, more than the amount of our personal philanthropy, which will bring about a brighter future for us in terms of our personal outlooks on life, and for our planet as a whole.

**7. Combating Hopelessness (yours, mine and ours)** – I hope at this point you're convinced that your charitable giving practiced as personal philanthropy can create in you a sense of serenity that will overcome any gloom and feelings of isolation you might be experiencing. This is how the act of giving strengthens the donor as much as – or even more than – the beneficiary.

Charitable giving additionally resonates on a larger scale because it brings about incremental change in everyone's mindsets. The more frequently that each of us gives, the more the cumulative positive effect increases – politically, socially and spiritually – to create a new and better reality that will combat the world's negativity and hopelessness.

After all, how can you feel negative and hopeless when you're saving the world?

**8. Feeling Good about Yourself** – Most charities will send you a written or emailed acknowledgement when you make a gift of money or time. Do this: take those notes of thanks and post them where you'll see them daily, like on your refrigerator, or the bathroom mirror…

That way, every day, you'll be reminded of the wonderful good that you're doing on behalf of others. And when you *are* reminded, take a moment to pause… create a visual image of how you've helped… and contemplate the change for the better that you've made. If you do this, I guarantee you'll feel good – no, *great* – about yourself.

How could you *not?*

**9. Self-Awareness** – Personal philanthropy begins when you learn how to *meditate* on your acts of giving (the way you might meditate on a mantra, or by counting your breaths). It is through this meditation on the good you're bringing about through charitable giving, that puts you in a more positive mindset, and also makes you increasingly self-aware.

The world's literature, mythology, spirituality and psychology tell us that there are many paths to enlightenment. However, every culture and religion agrees on one thing: that enlightenment begins and ends with *self-awareness.*

You will be more self-aware in the most positive way when you meditate on how you are helping others and the world through your personal philanthropy.

**10. Realizing How Good You Have It… *no matter what 'It' is!*** – All of us confront problems and challenges in life. We may be struggling with personal, financial or health issues. We may feel like there's no way to escape our utter depression and despair.

Your practice of personal philanthropy will help you put your own problems in perspective as you focus on the needs of others. In this way, your meditation on your altruism can cast a light on your difficulties, shrinking them down to size and banishing the shadows.

All that's required of you is to contemplate the wonderful difference you are making through your personal philanthropy – and realize you deserve to feel good about it.

This is *How to Save the World on $5 a Day.*

# ABOUT THE AUTHOR

Fred Lawrence Feldman has published under various pseudonyms seventeen hardcover and paperback original novels. Many have also been published internationally.

Fred has also been a successful direct marketing creative consultant, partnering with nonprofit organizations for over twenty years. His award-winning fundraising communications strategies and executions have helped to raise millions of dollars on behalf of many well-known national charities.

A Fifth Degree Black Belt in Uechi-Ryu karate, Fred credits his martial arts training for greatly contributing to his personal journey toward melding mind, body and spirit. His years spent in the dojo – learning and teaching – have helped him refine many of the ideas he shares in *How to Save the World on $5 a Day.*

He lives with his wife in Massachusetts, north of Boston.